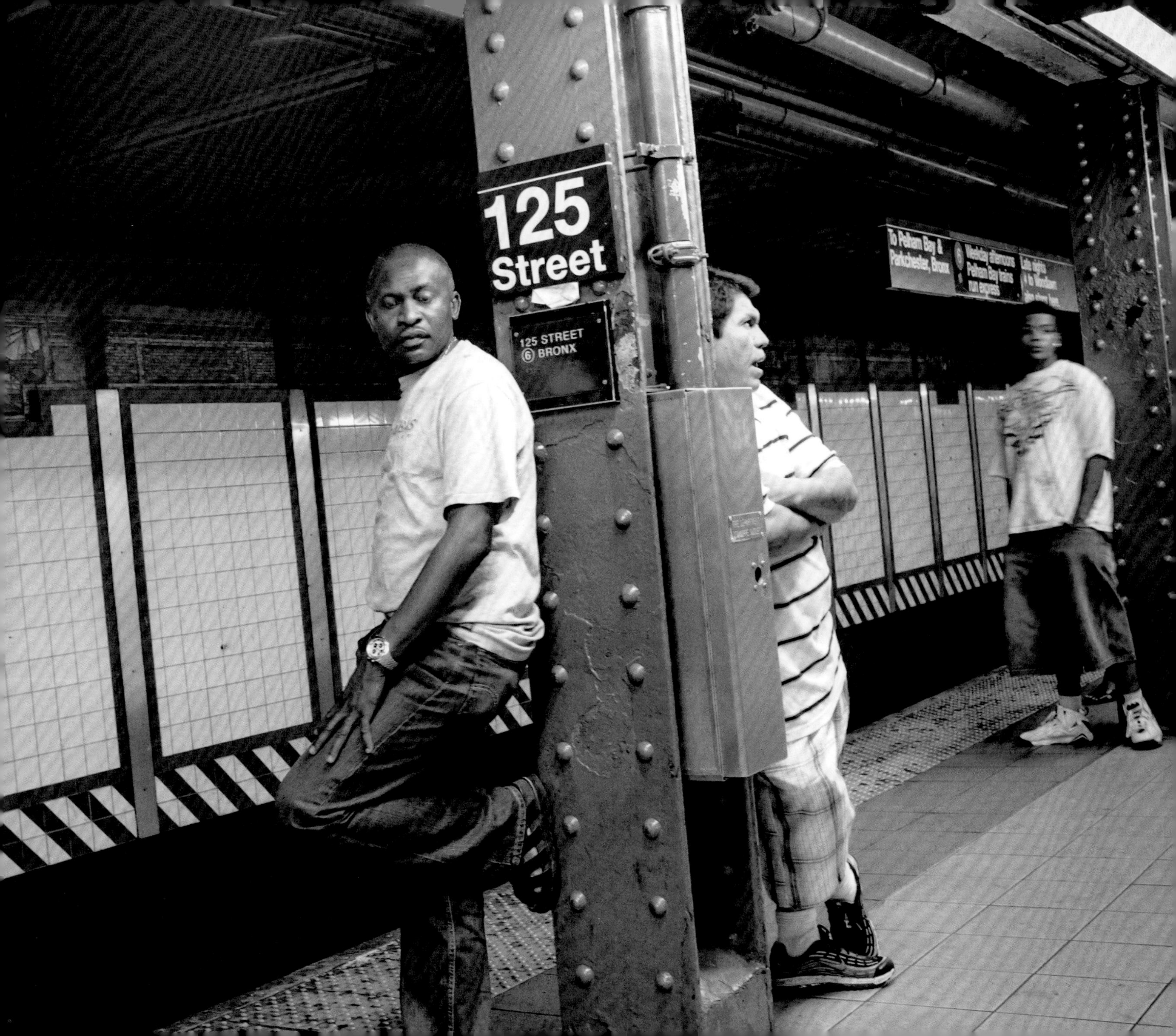
125
Street
125 STREET
6 BRONX
To Pelham Bay &
Parkchester, Bronx
Weekday afternoons
Pelham Bay trains
run express

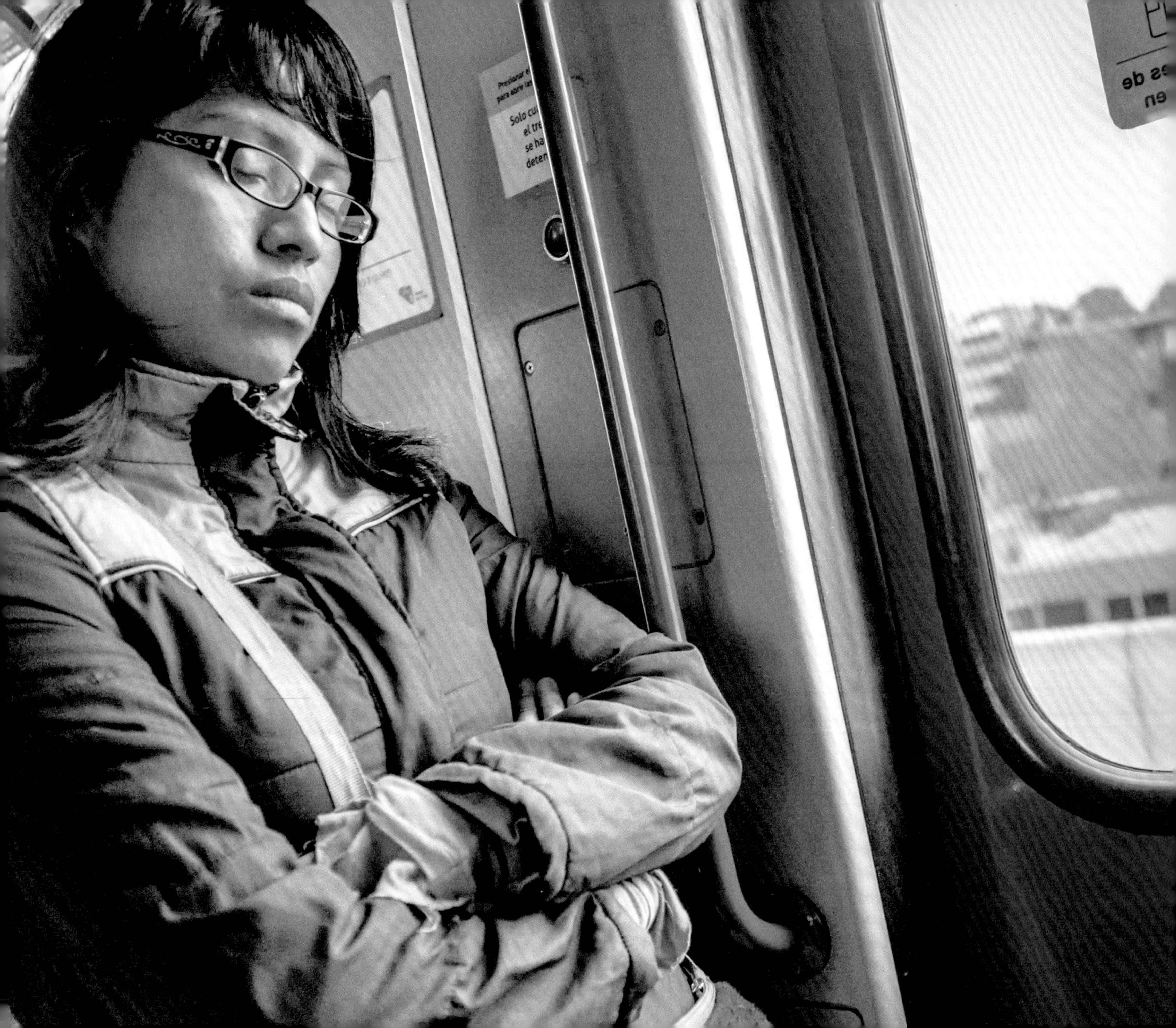

METRO

Cofounders: Taj Forer and Michael Itkoff
Designer: Ursula Damm
Copy editor: Elizabeth Bell

ISBN 978-1-942084-15-0

Printed in Turkey

Daylight Books
E-mail: info@daylightbooks.org
Web: www.daylightbooks.org

Stan Raucher

METRO

Scenes from an Urban Stage

Daylight

Stan Raucher has spent countless hours underground over the past eight years. He hasn't been hiding out or avoiding the world. In fact, he's been keenly observing and gracefully documenting the social landscape of subway systems in more than a dozen cities around the globe. Whether in Paris, New York, London, Delhi, São Paulo, or Mexico City, his sensitive eye has recorded with an athlete's discipline and rigor the many human interactions that go unheralded, or even shunned, by most people traveling through these crowded public spaces.

Metro: Scenes from an Urban Stage explores the mass of humanity passing through this subterranean realm. I've seen many photographic treatments of this subject, but what makes Stan's images valuable and unique is the scope, quality, and humanity they possess. There is a lovely candid essence to so many of his photos—like the image of the two women on the Piccadilly Line in London joyfully hugging while sandwiched between the usual glum expressions so often seen on the metro, or the raw emotion displayed between the couple on the Blue Line in Delhi. Stan's camera is seemingly invisible while recording these fleeting exchanges.

It's a funny thing about riding the subway. We inhabit a relatively small, intimate space with strangers. We bring our literal and figurative baggage there, trying to get from one point to another. Sometimes it's for pleasurable activities, but more often than not it's a utilitarian ride, accompanied by our anxieties, fatigue, expectations, and, at times, fears. Stan's images reveal these qualities and something more nuanced—they allow us a glimpse into the psyches of the people involved. The richness and depth of his black-and-white photography add an important element to this work. It enhances the emotional content and forces the viewer to dwell that much longer to absorb the textures of the scenes he has so adeptly captured.

As I look at the images in this book, one reaction remains constant—I want to know more about the people and what was actually going on in that moment. That is the magic of still photography. It forces us to ask questions, to wonder, to meditate, and to think. This book is part of a great legacy of photographic work that has been produced about subway passengers. Possibly the first was done by Walker Evans incognito in the 1930s, to be carried forward by Bruce Davidson in color 50 years later in the 1980s. And now we have Stan Raucher's modern-day version. This is something to see, to ponder, and to cherish.

—Ed Kashi

Stare.
It is the way to educate your eye, and more.
Stare, pry, listen, eavesdrop.
Die knowing something.
You are not here long.

—*Walker Evans*

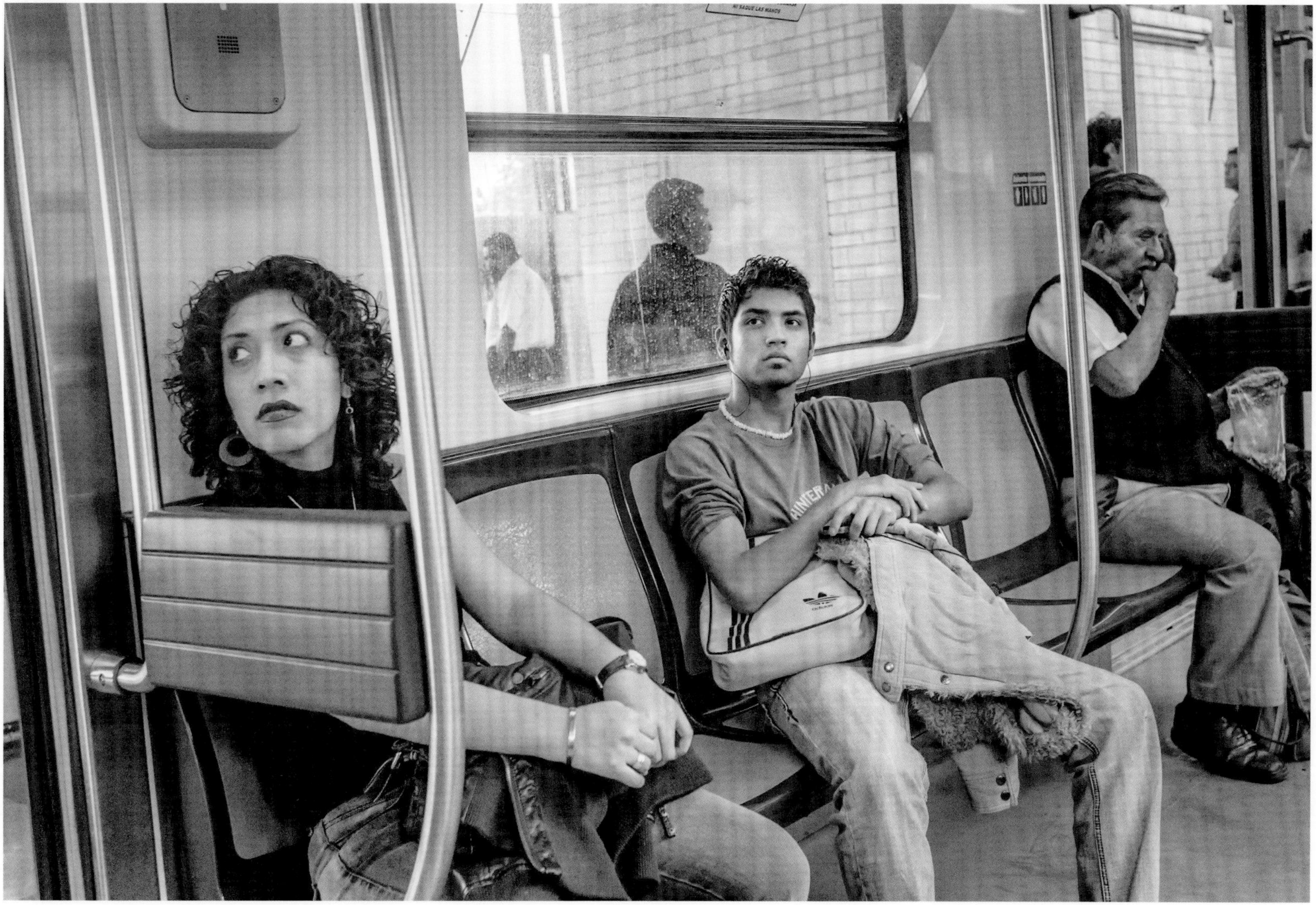

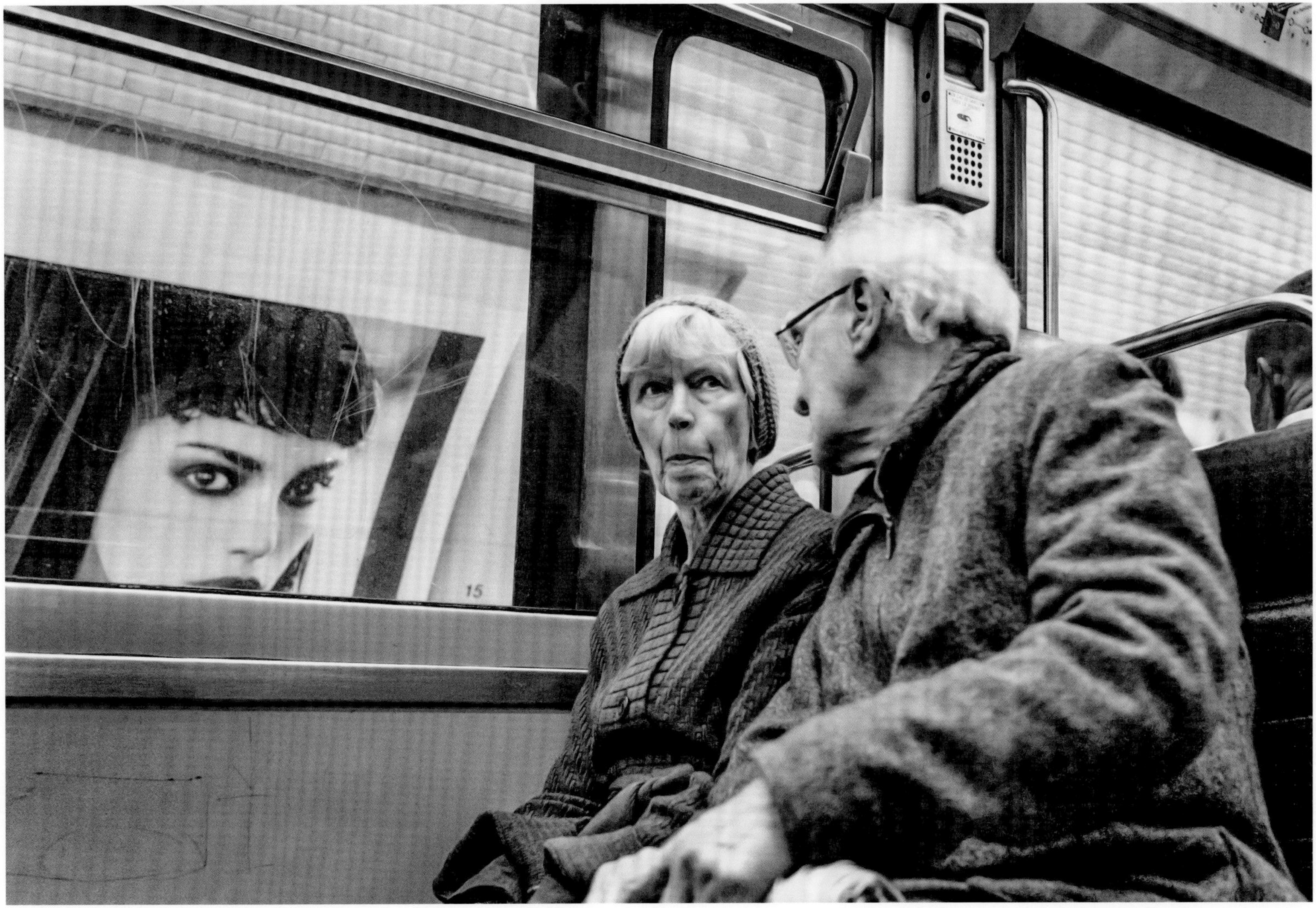

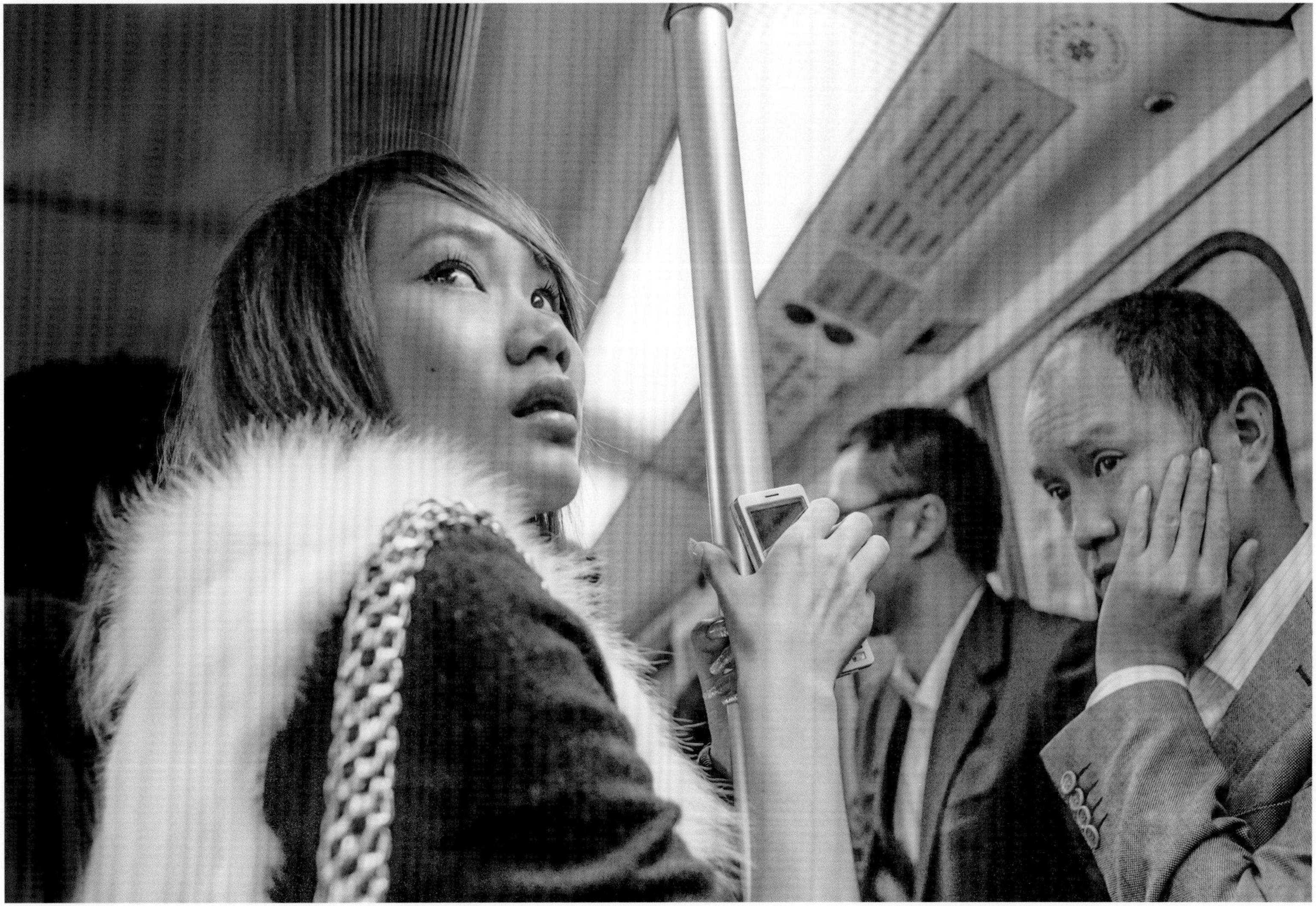

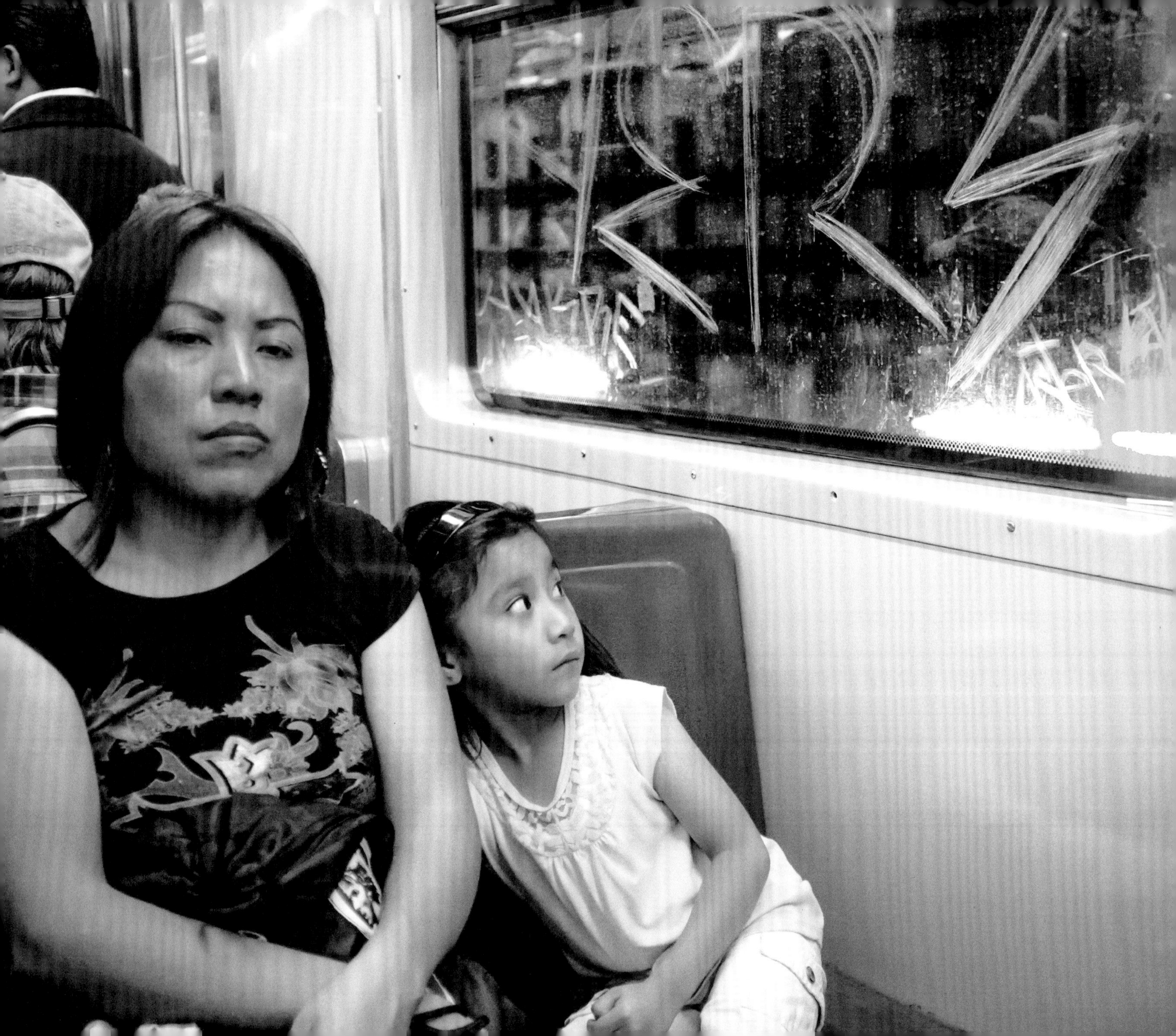

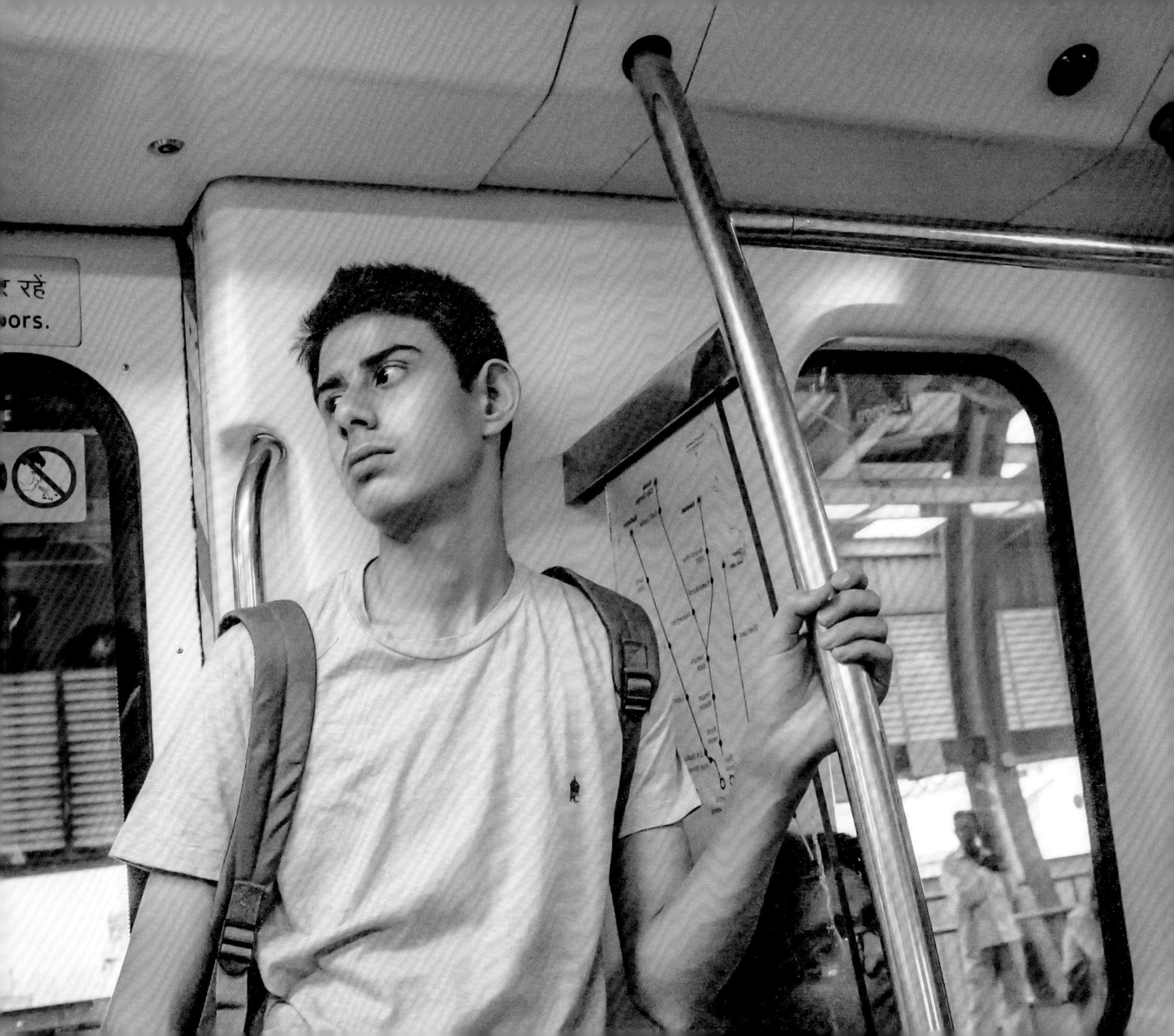

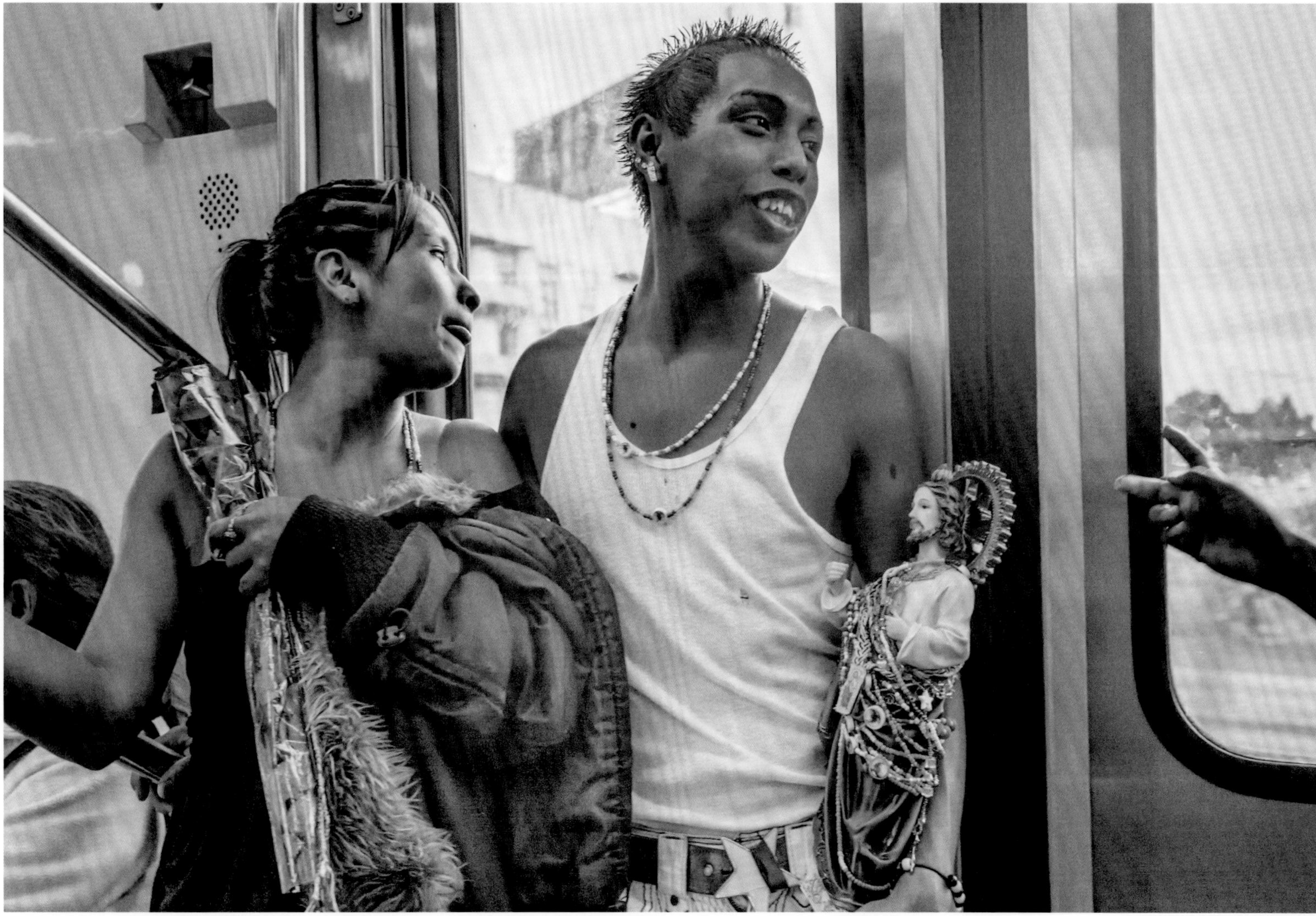

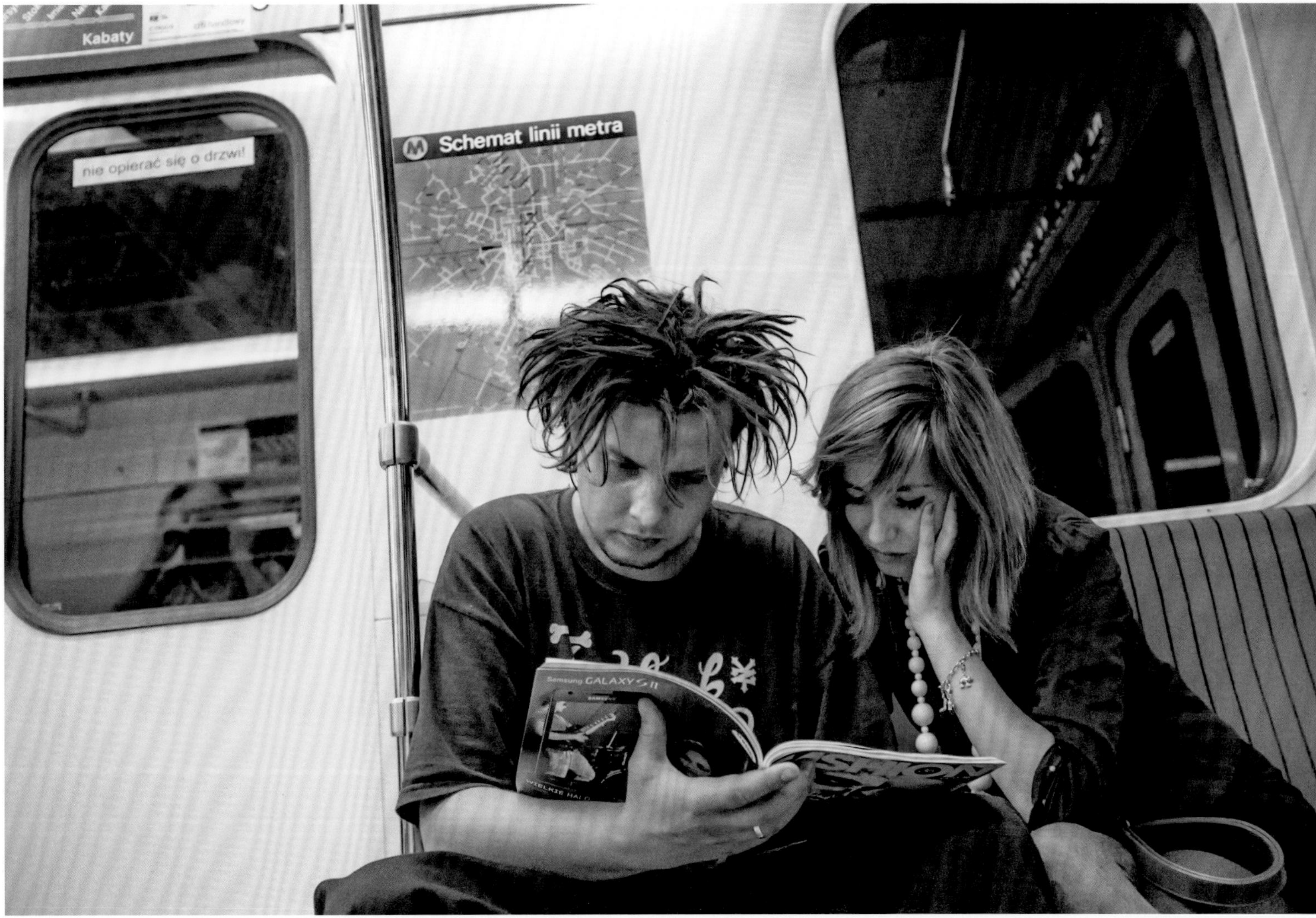
Kabaty
nie opierać się o drzwi!
Schemat linii metra
Samsung GALAXY S II

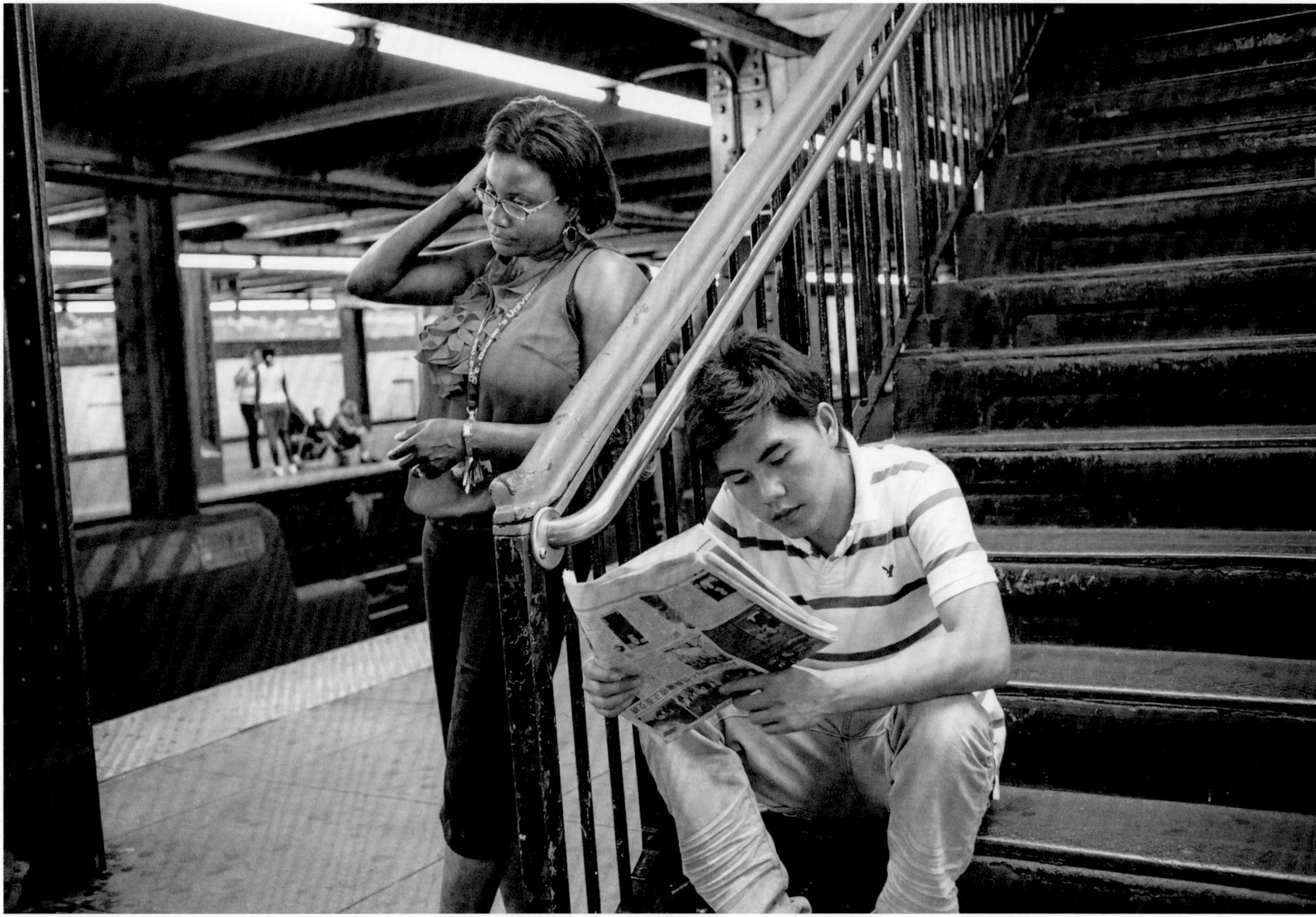

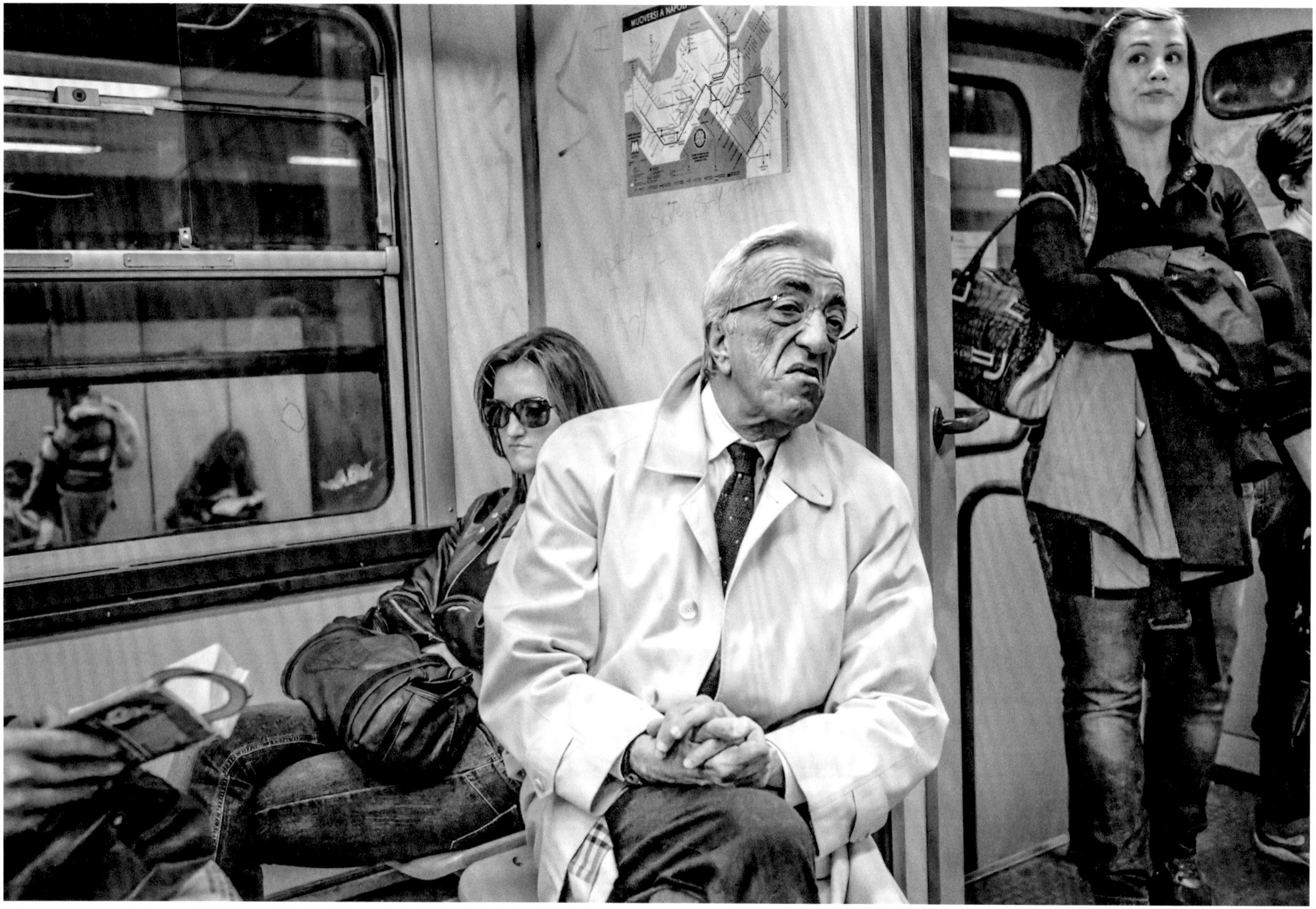
MUOVERSI A

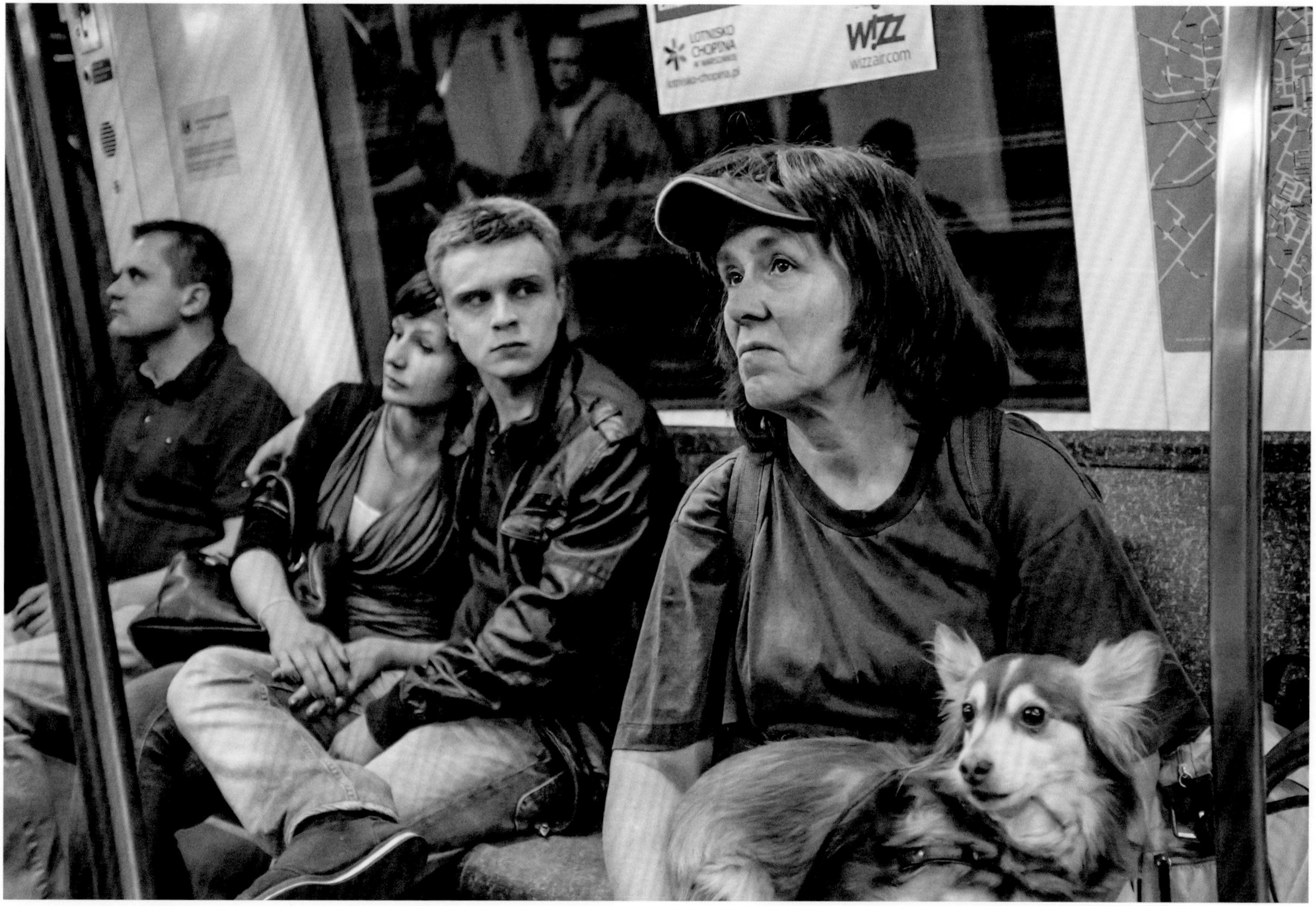
LOTNISKO CHOPINA
W!ZZ
wizzair.com

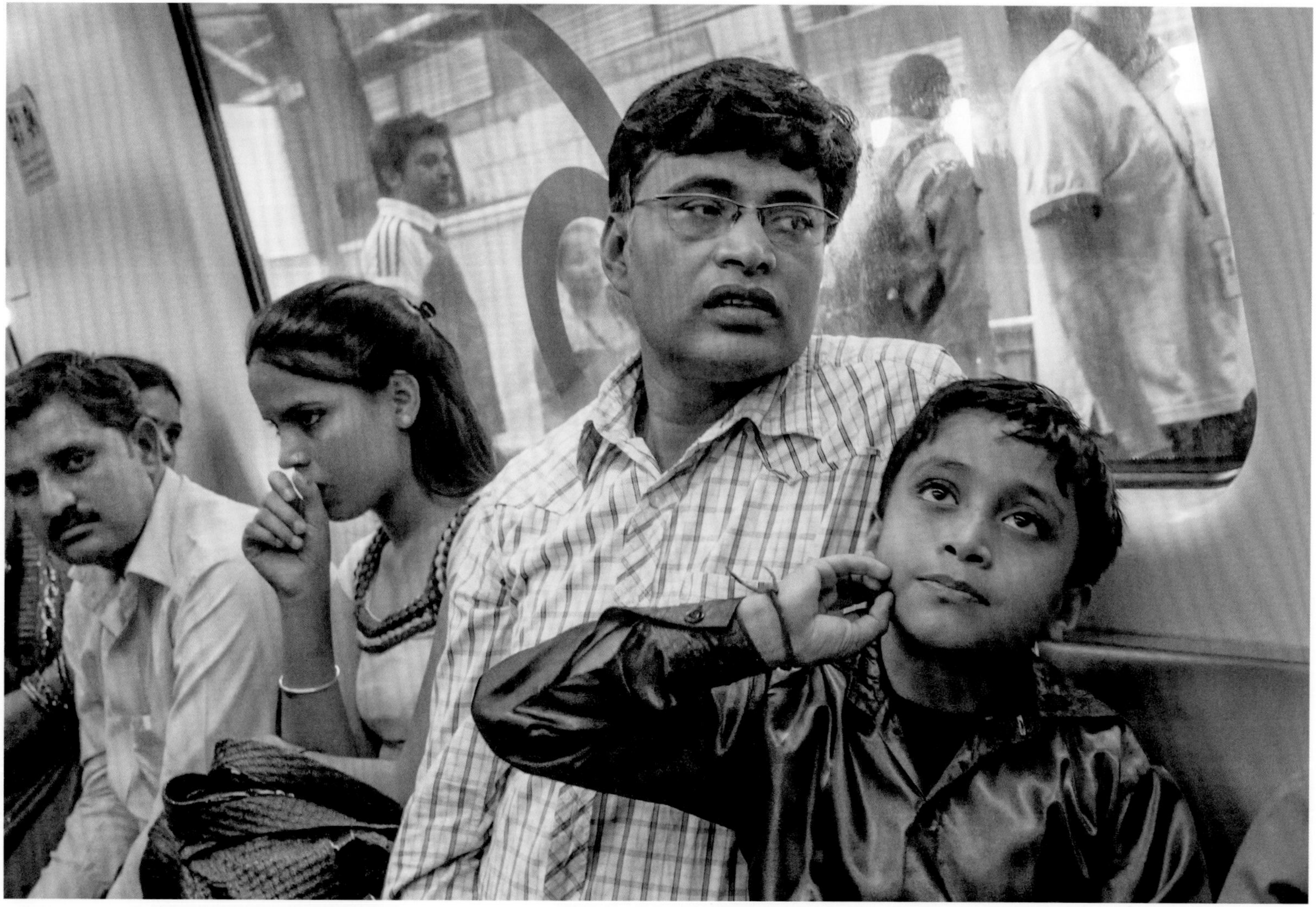

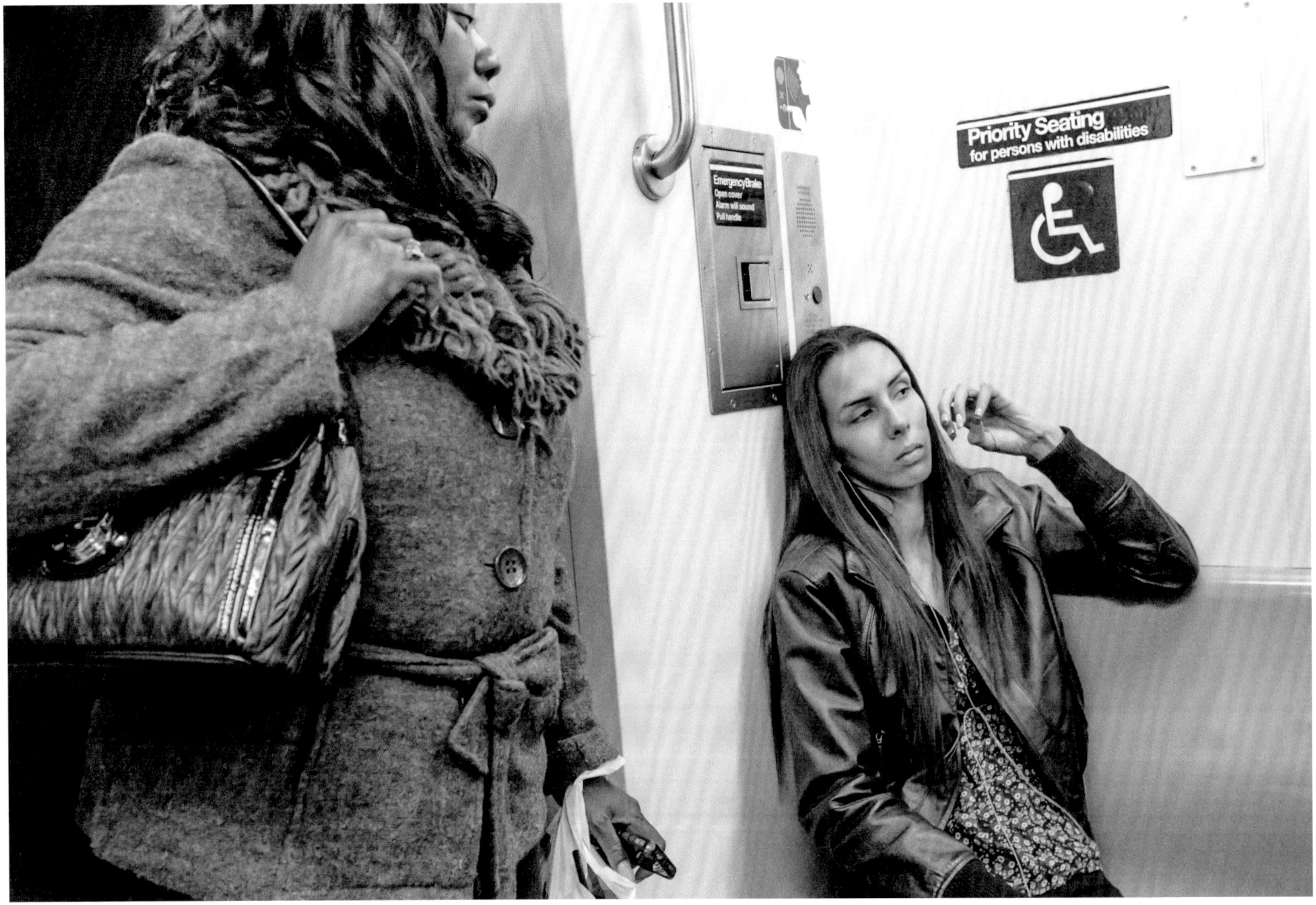
Emergency Brake
Open cover
Alarm will sound
Pull handle
Priority Seating
for persons with disabilities

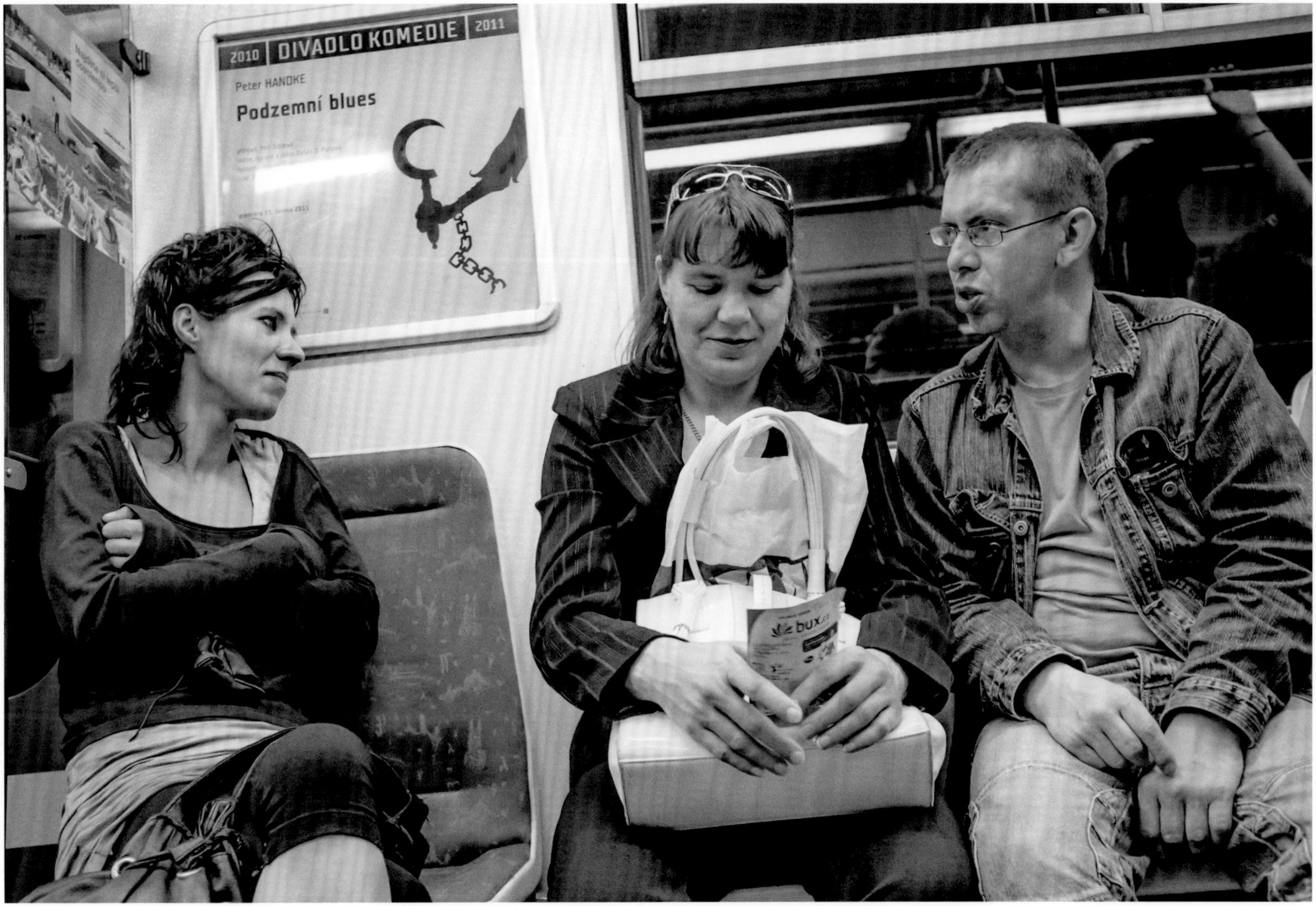
2010
DIVADLO KOMEDIE
2011
Peter HANDKE
Podzemní blues

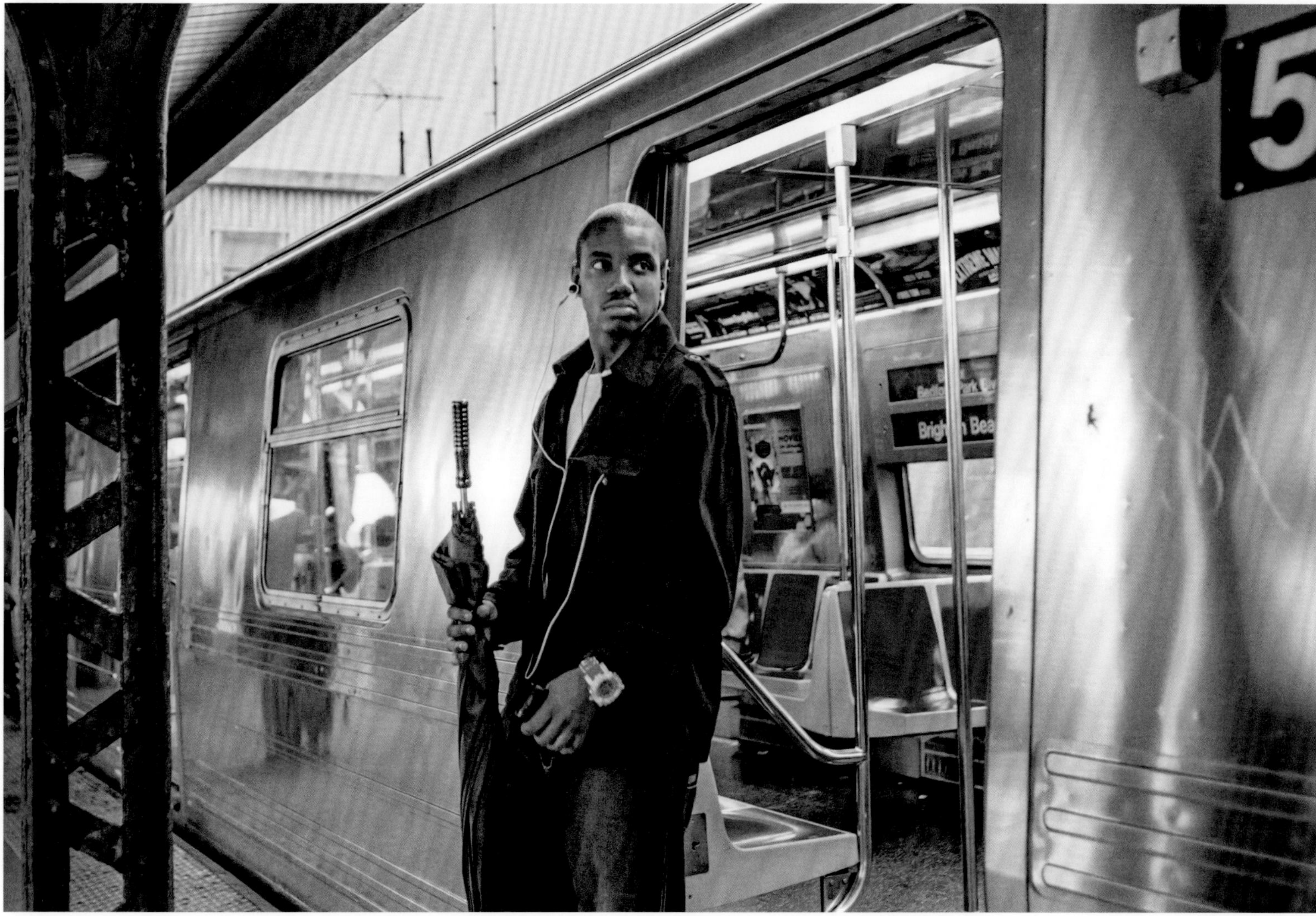
5

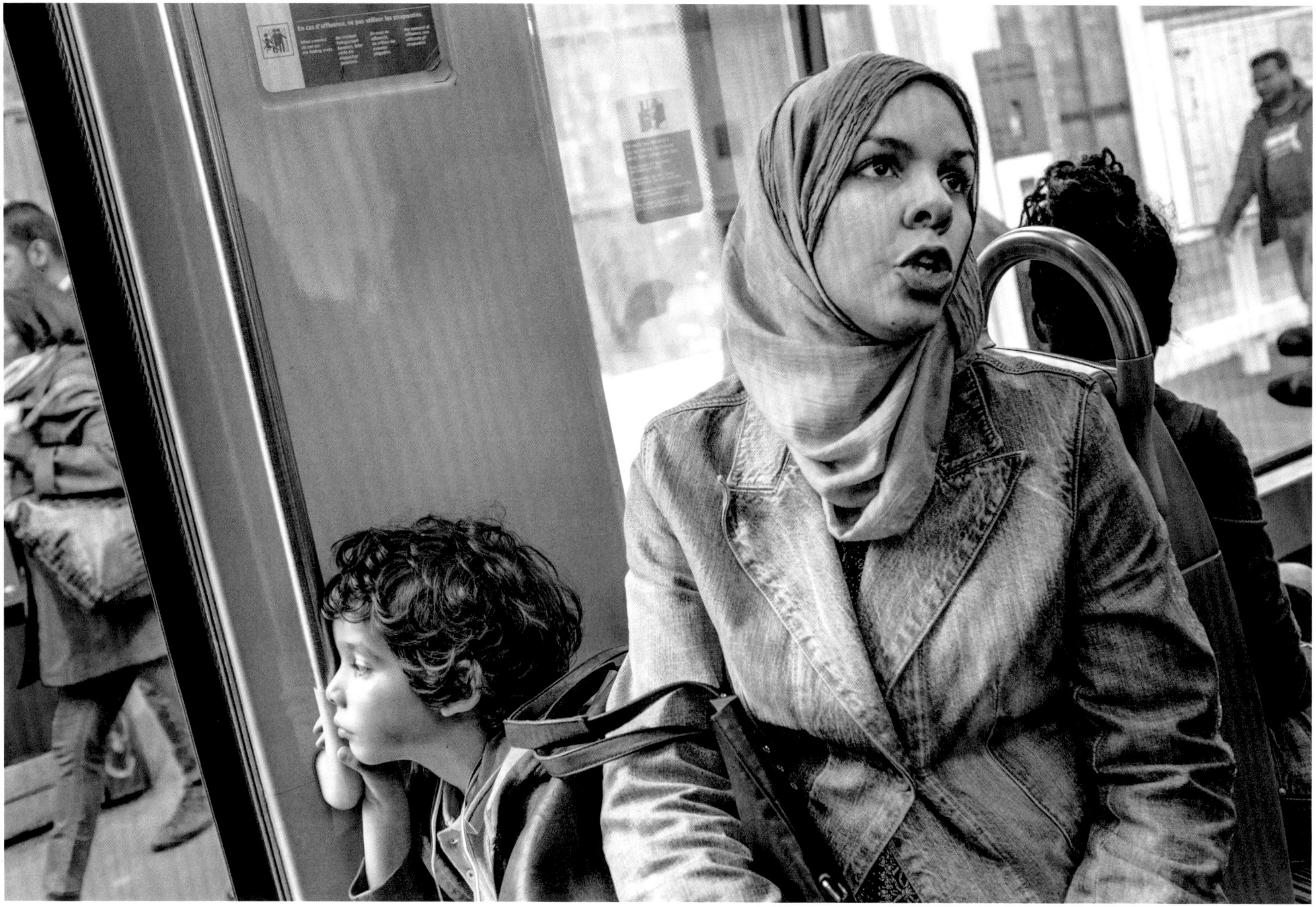
En cas d'affluence, ne pas utiliser les strapontins.

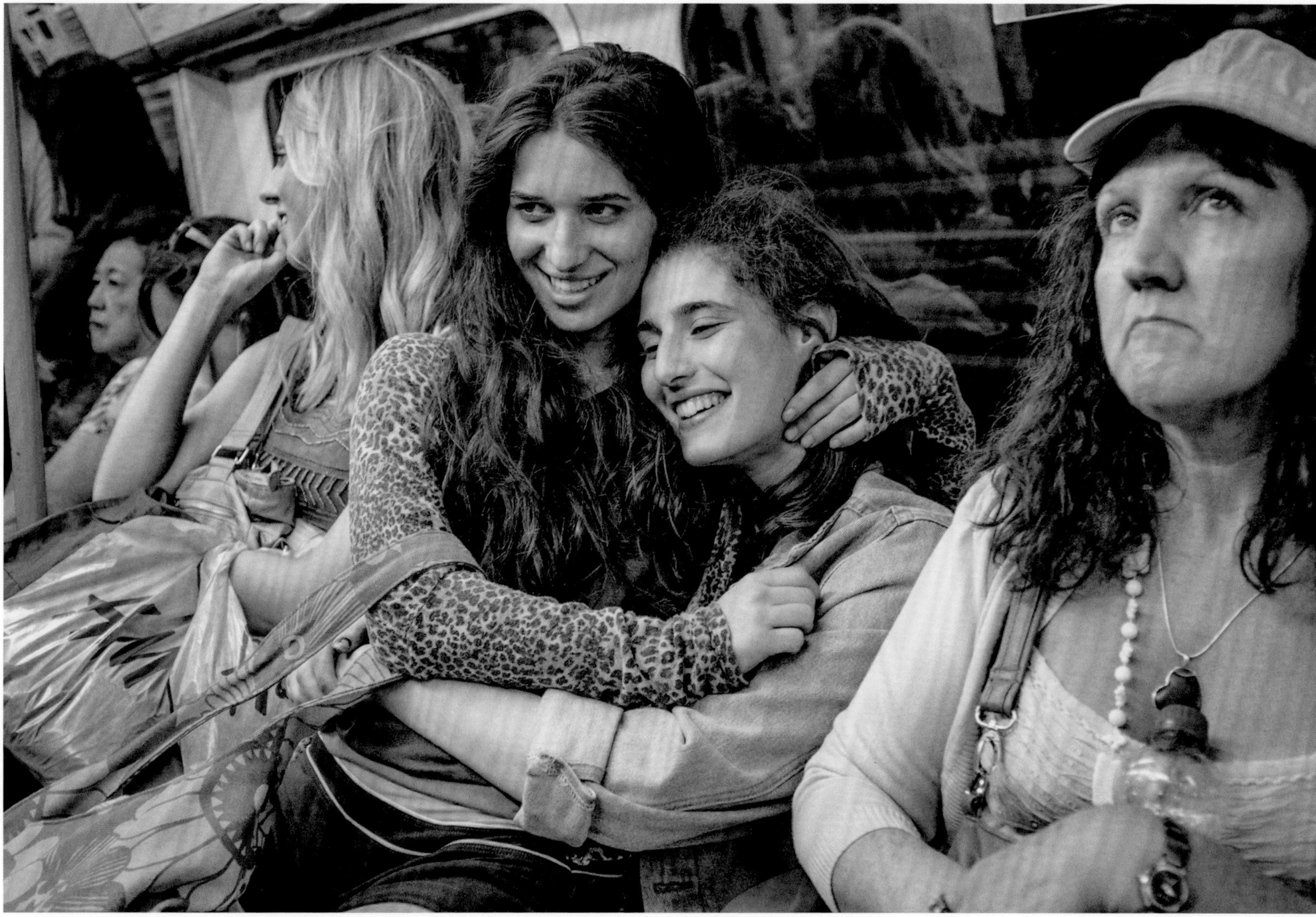

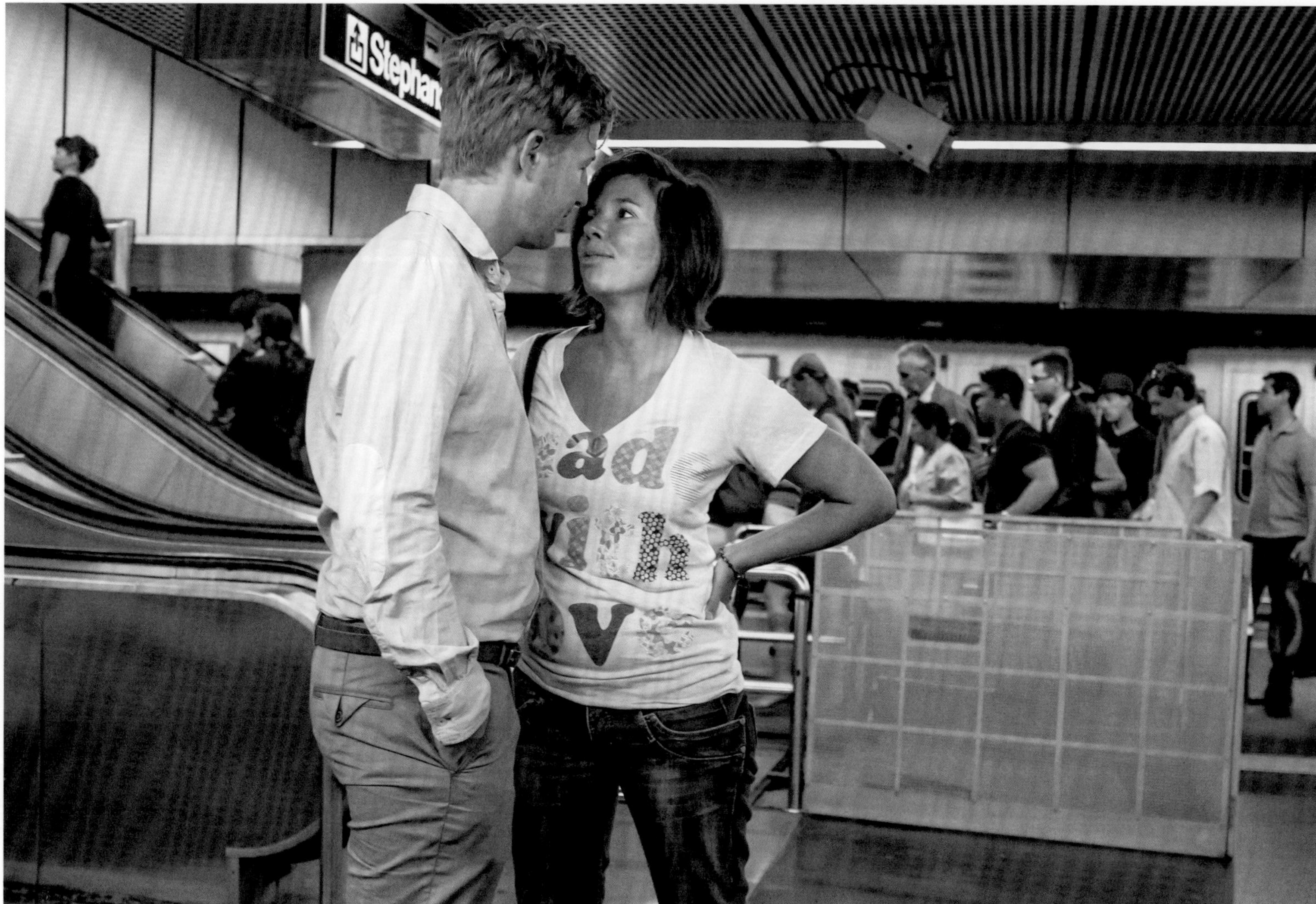

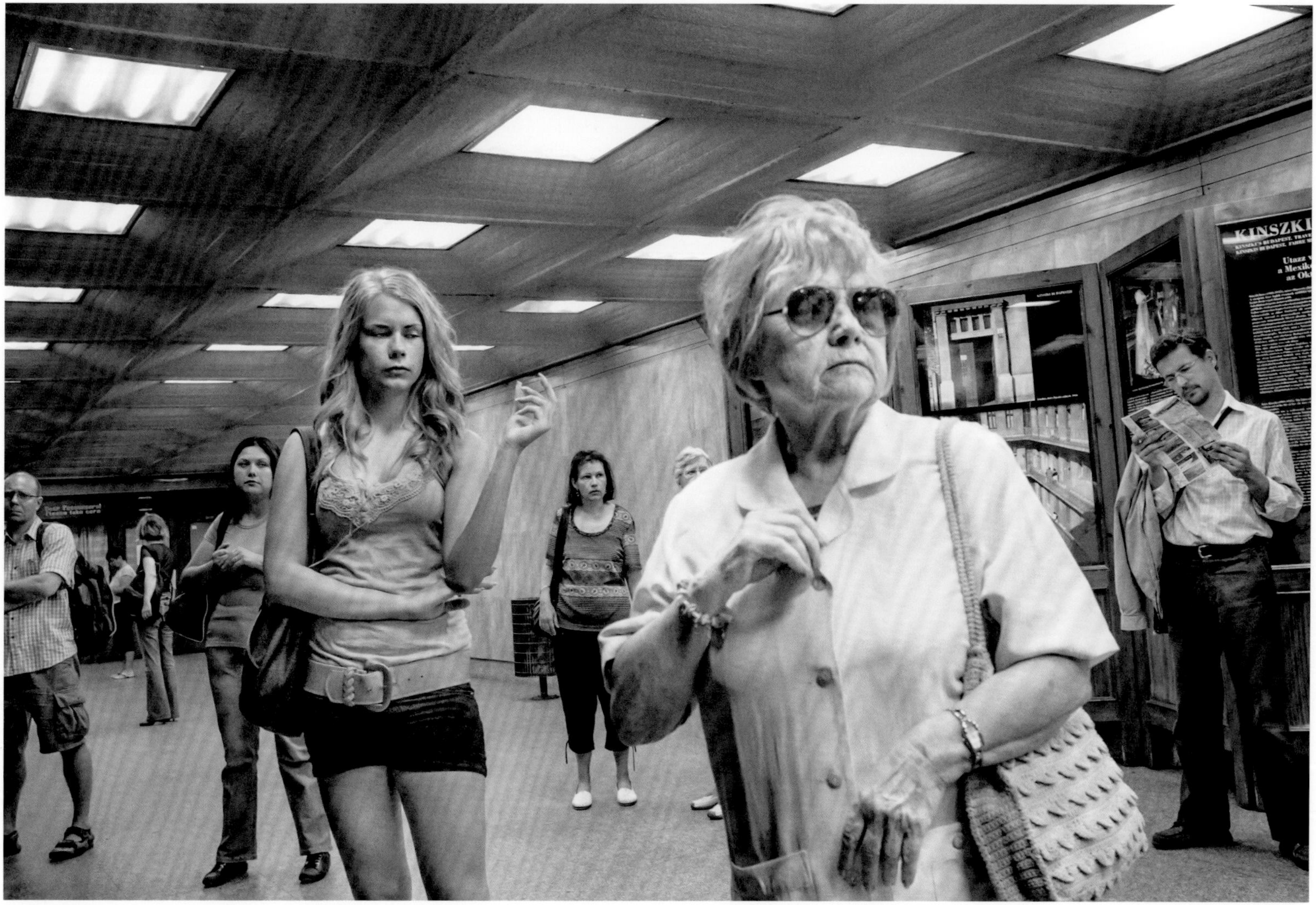

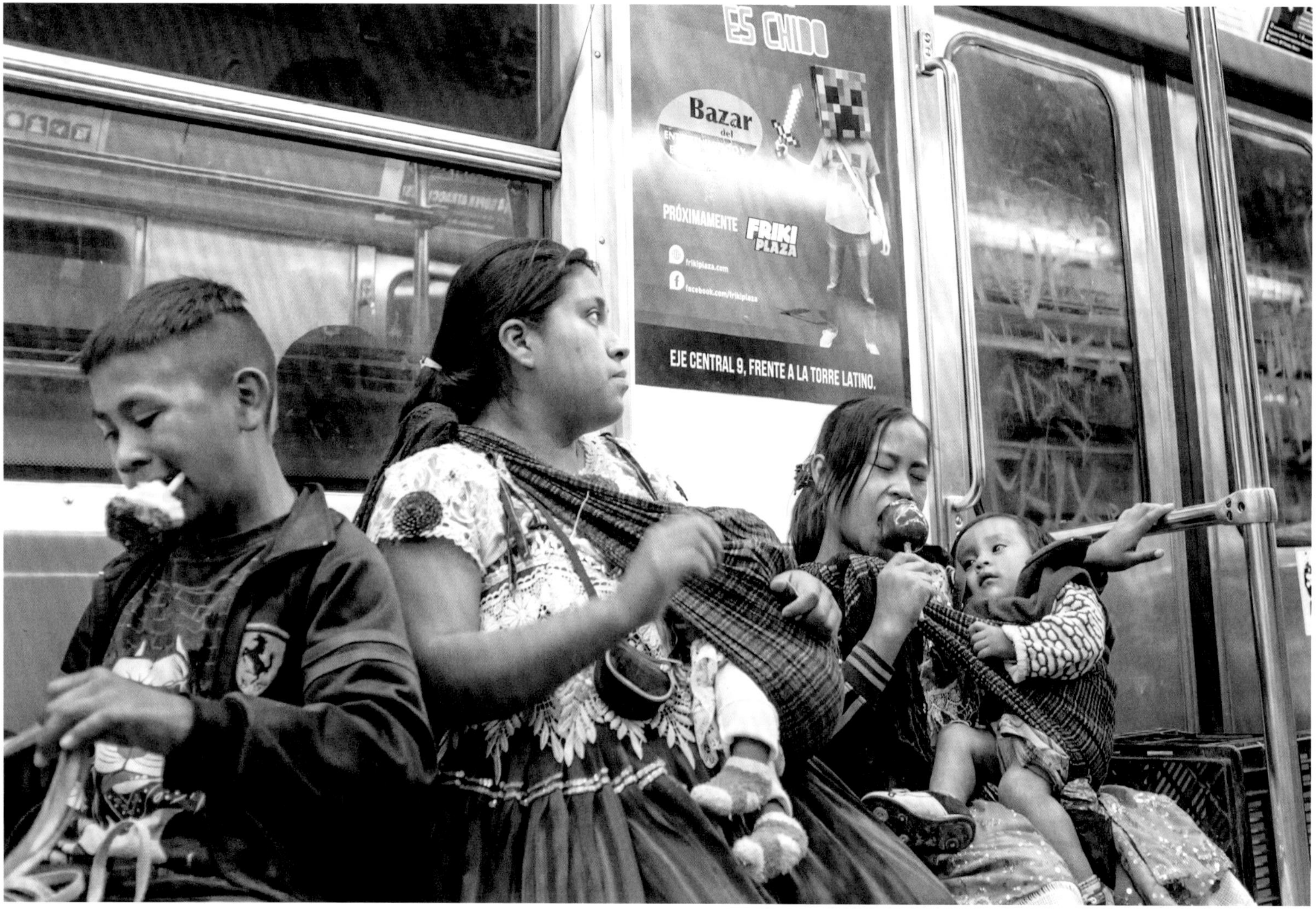
ES CHIDO
Bazar
PRÓXIMAMENTE
FRIKI PLAZA
EJE CENTRAL 9, FRENTE A LA TORRE LATINO.

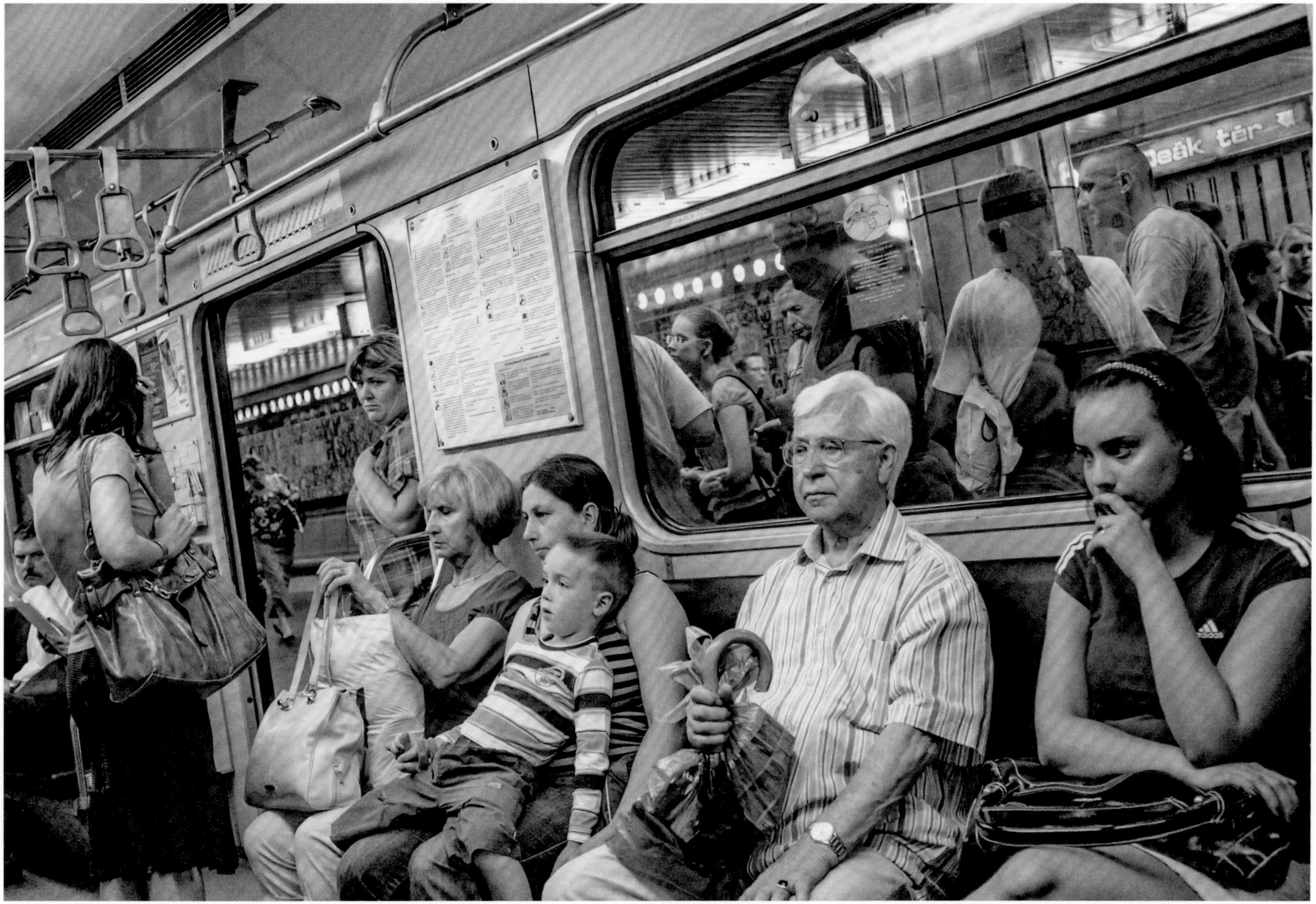
tér
adidas

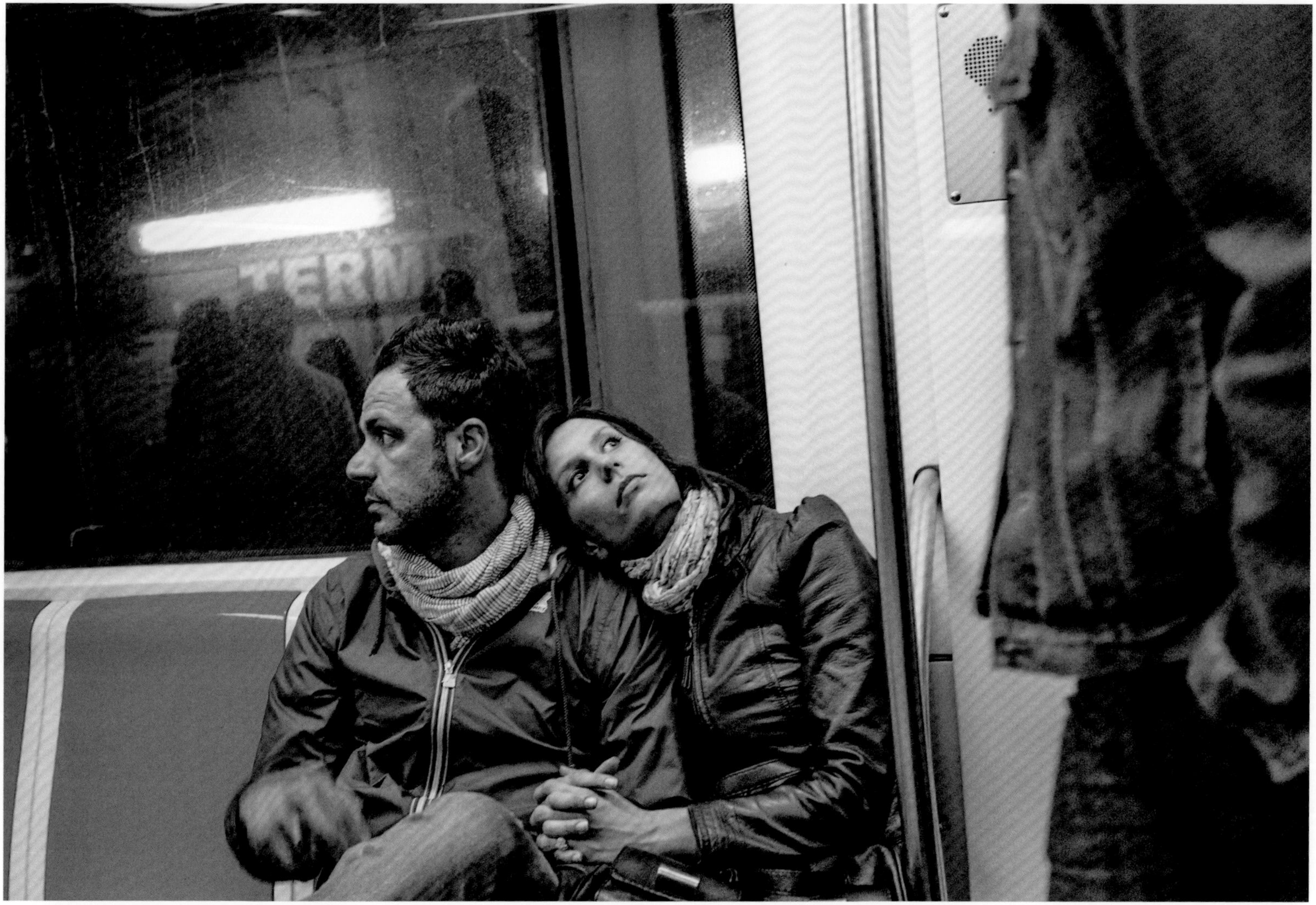
TERM

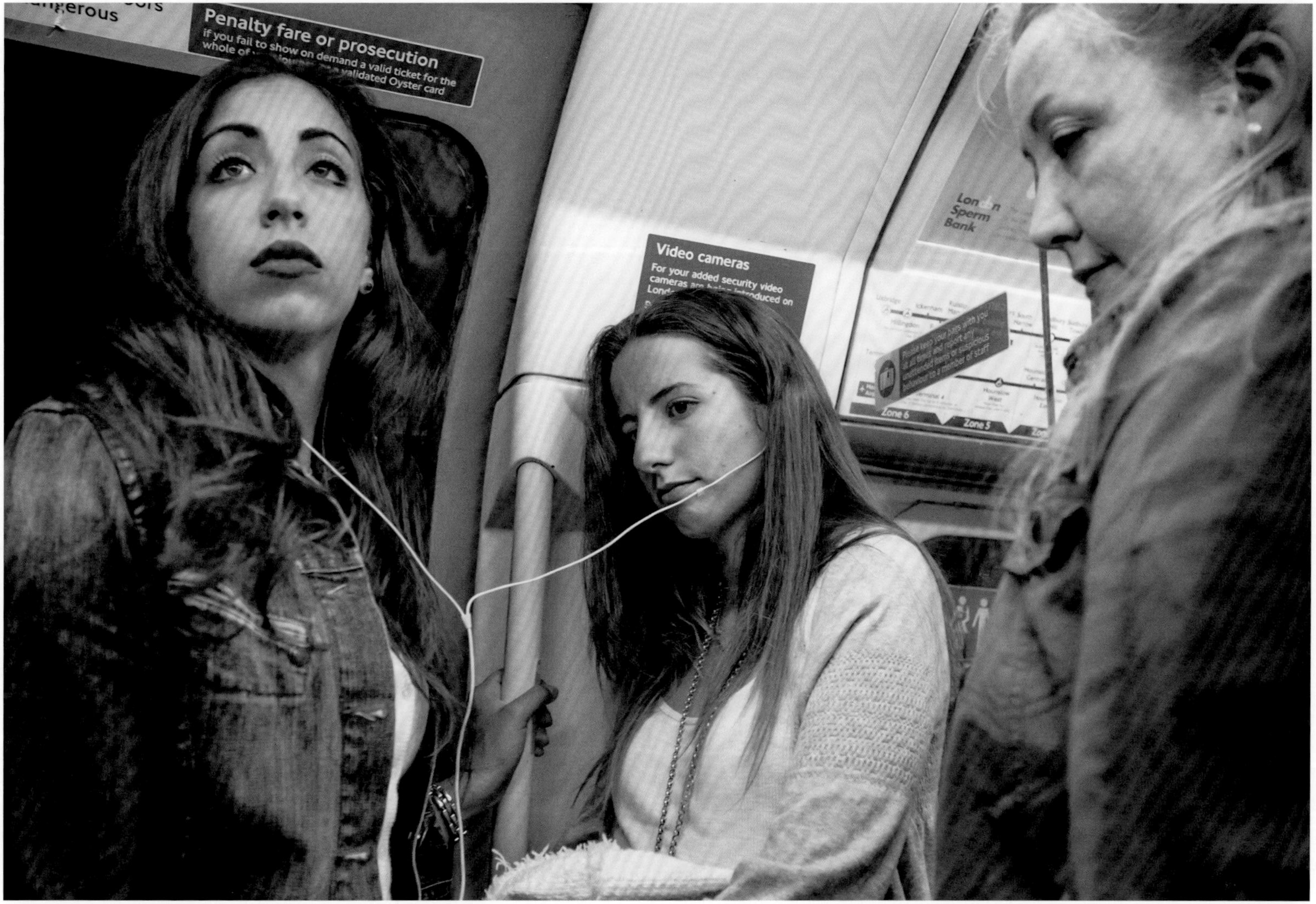
Penalty fare or prosecution
if you fail to show on demand a valid ticket for the
Video cameras
For your added security video
Sperm
Bank
Zone 6
Zone 5

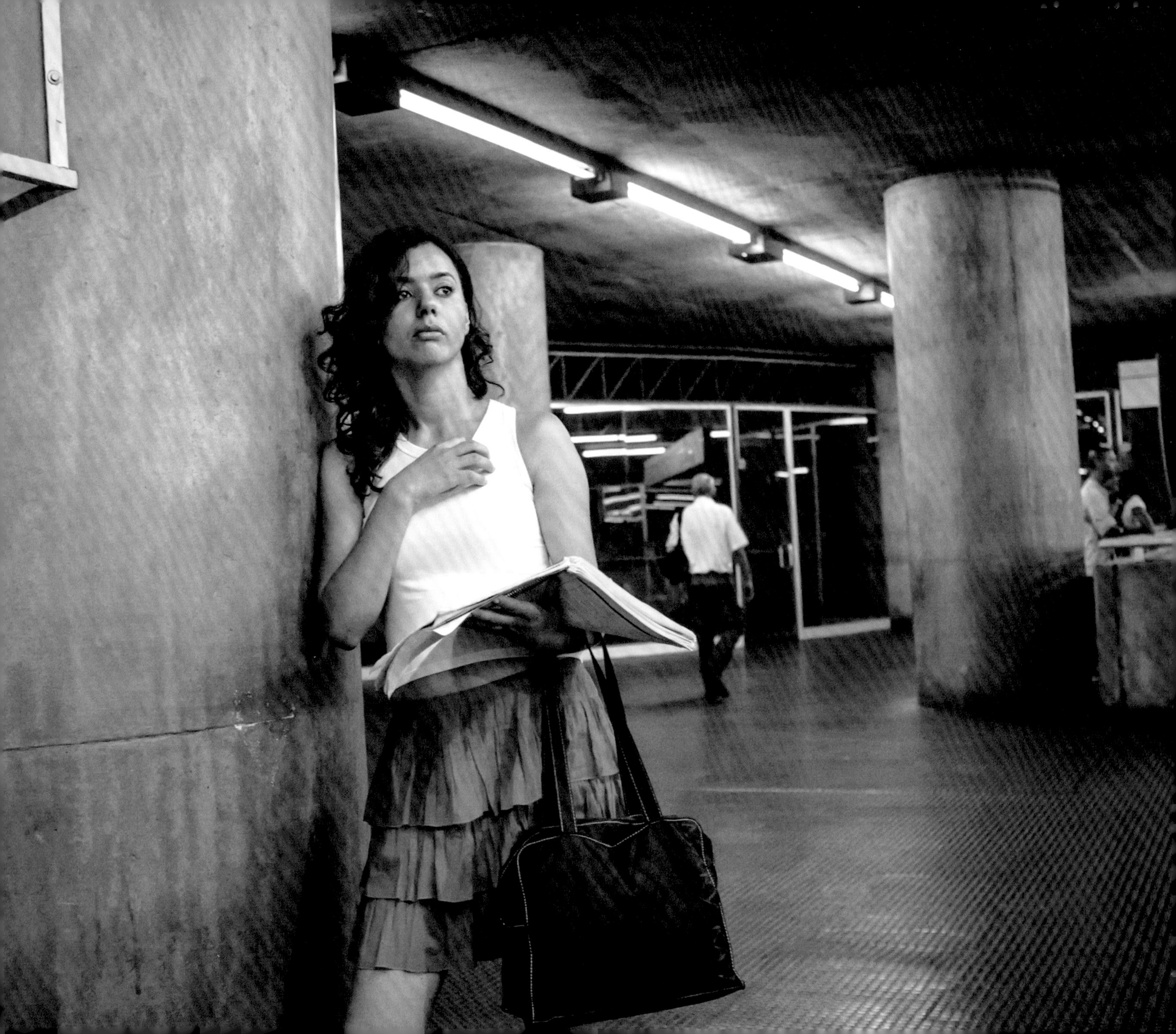

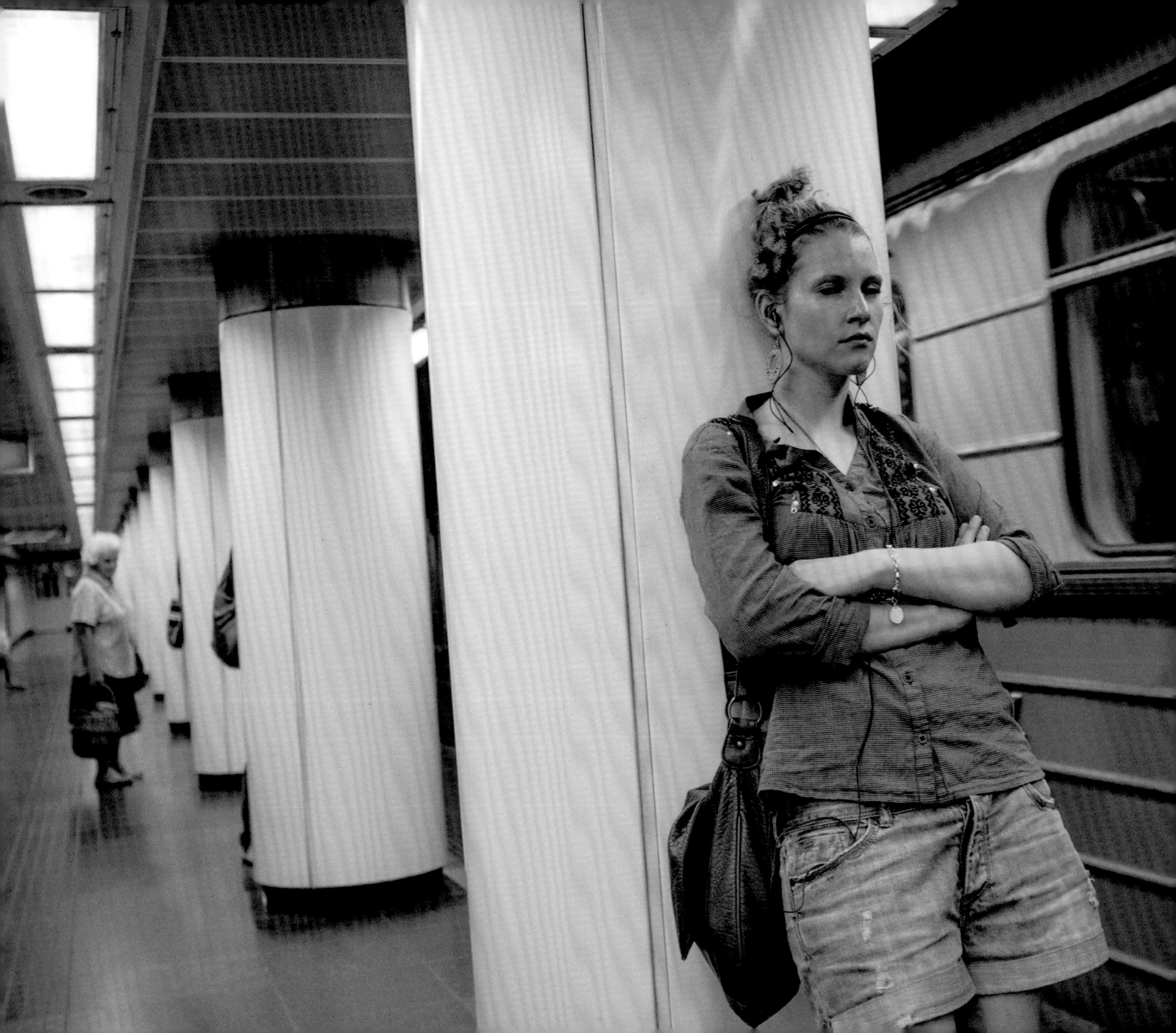

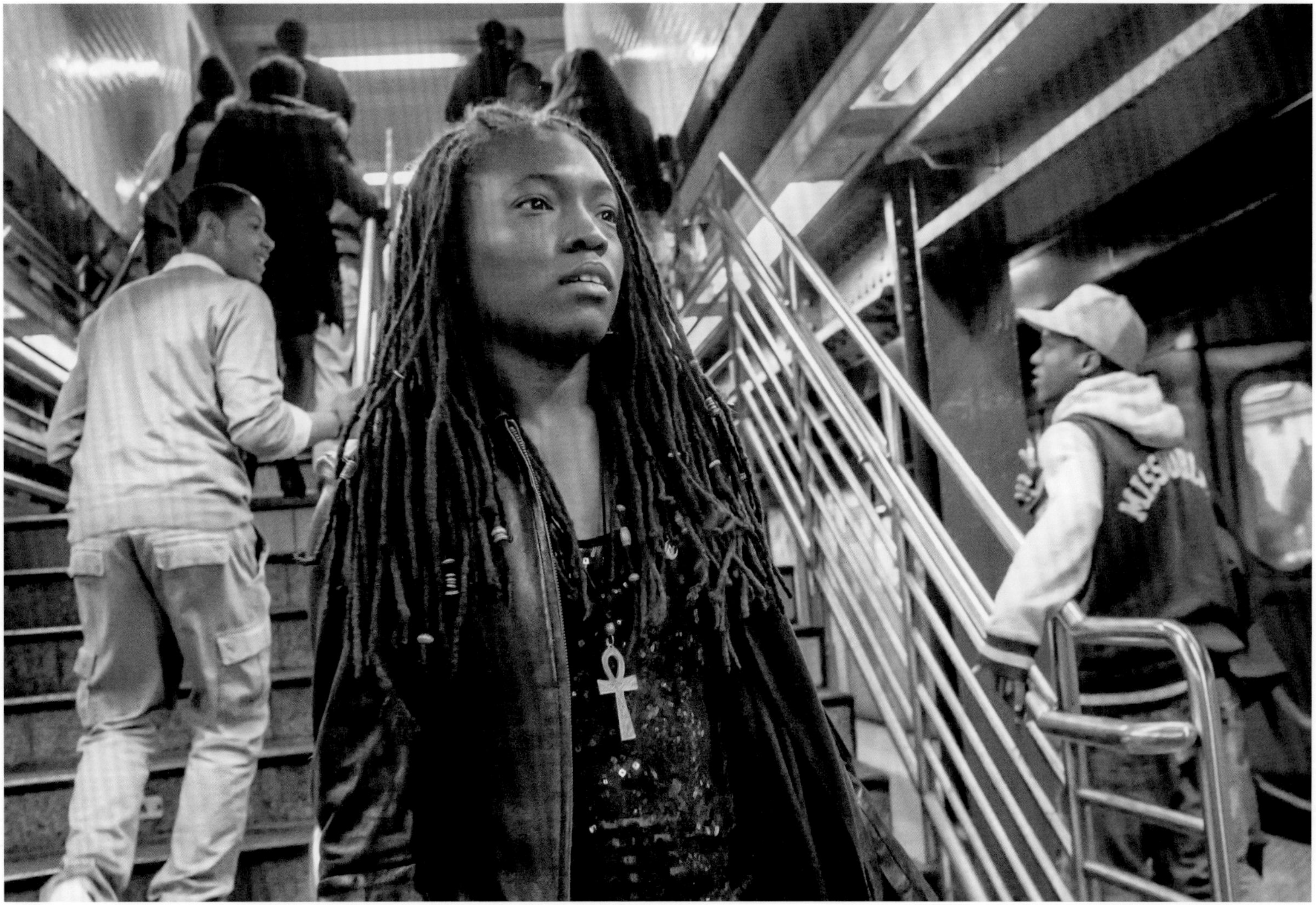

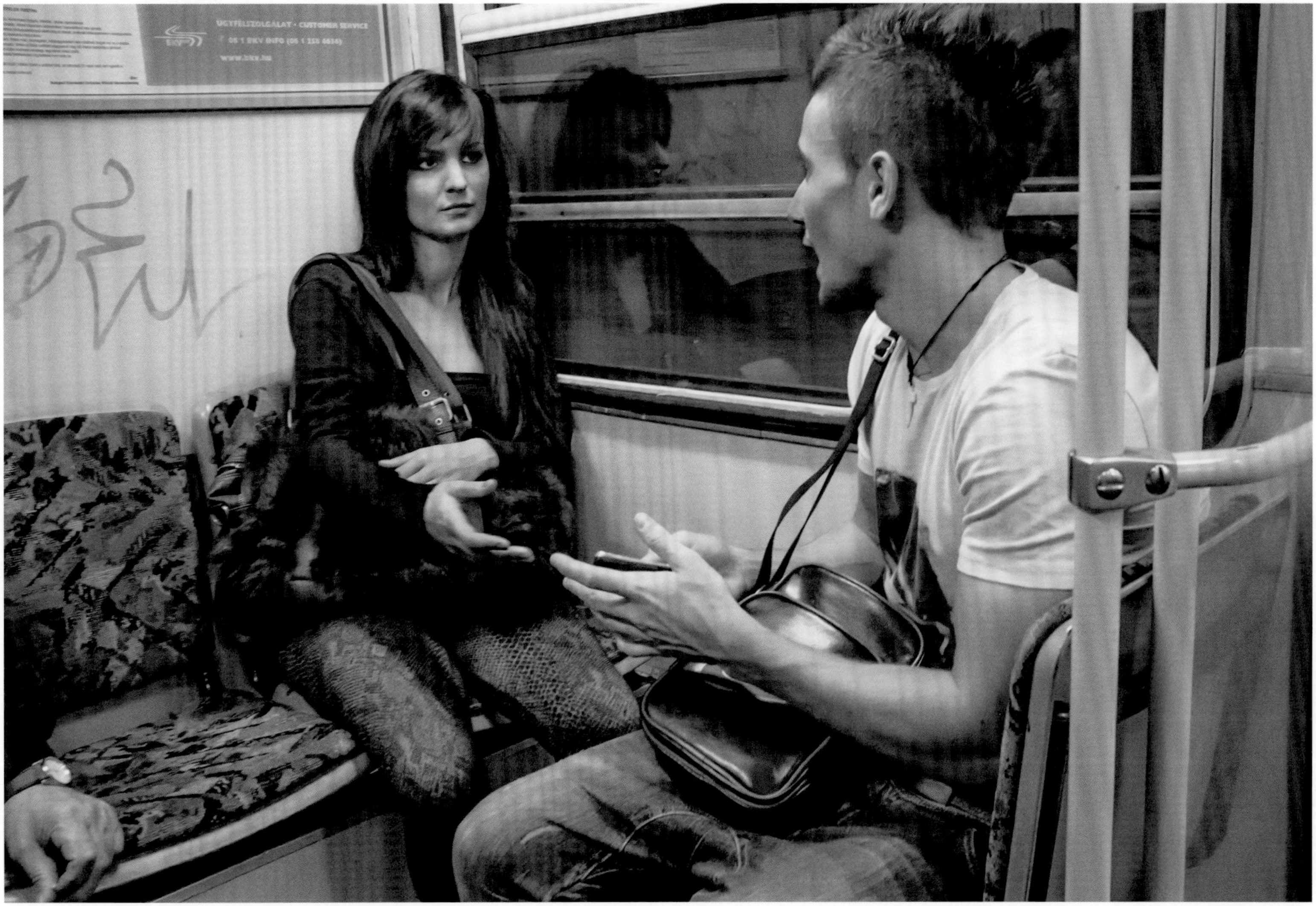
ÜGYFÉLSZOLGÁLAT • CUSTOMER SERVICE
www.bkv.hu

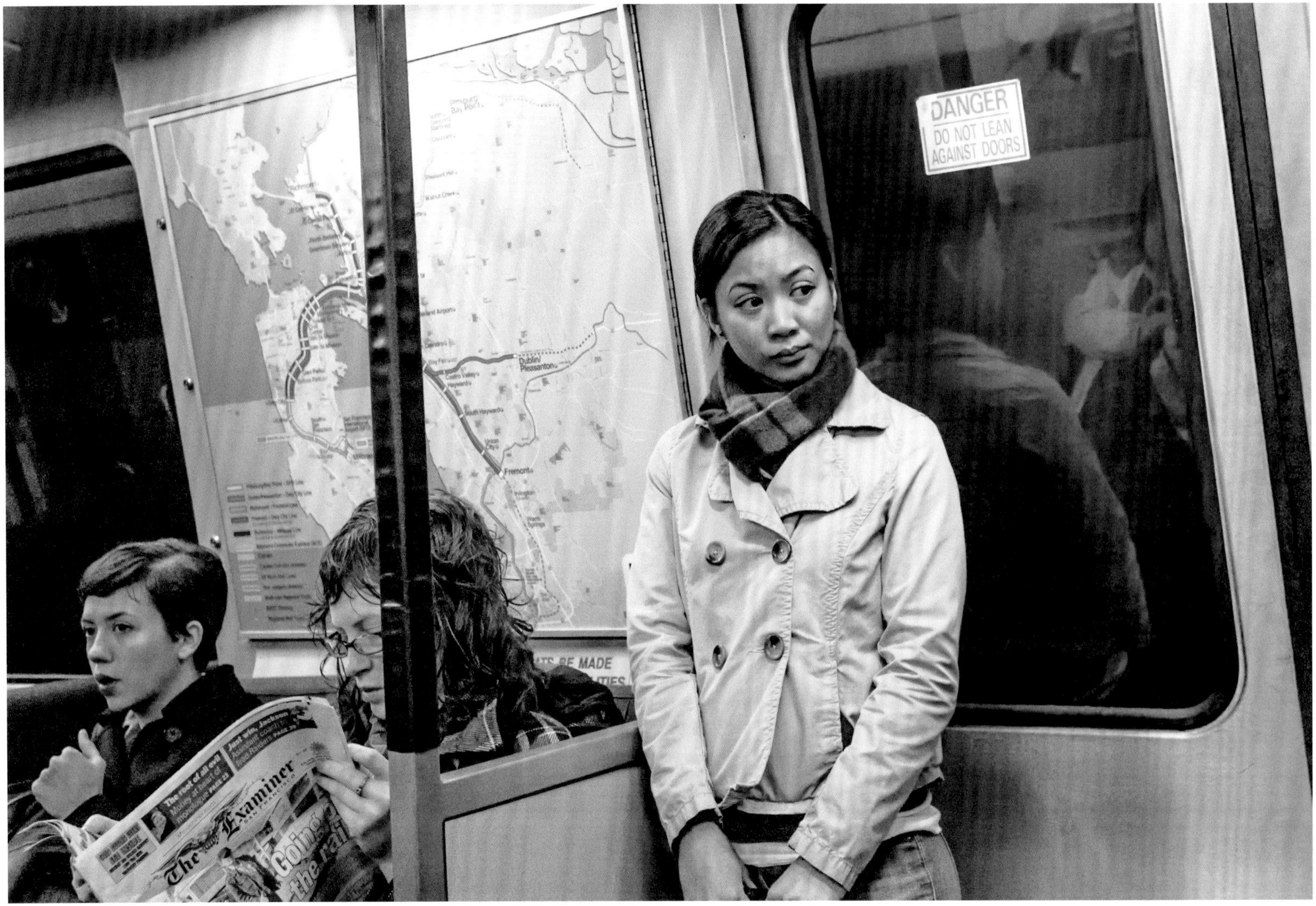
DANGER
DO NOT LEAN
AGAINST DOORS
The Examiner
Dublin/
Pleasanton
Fremont

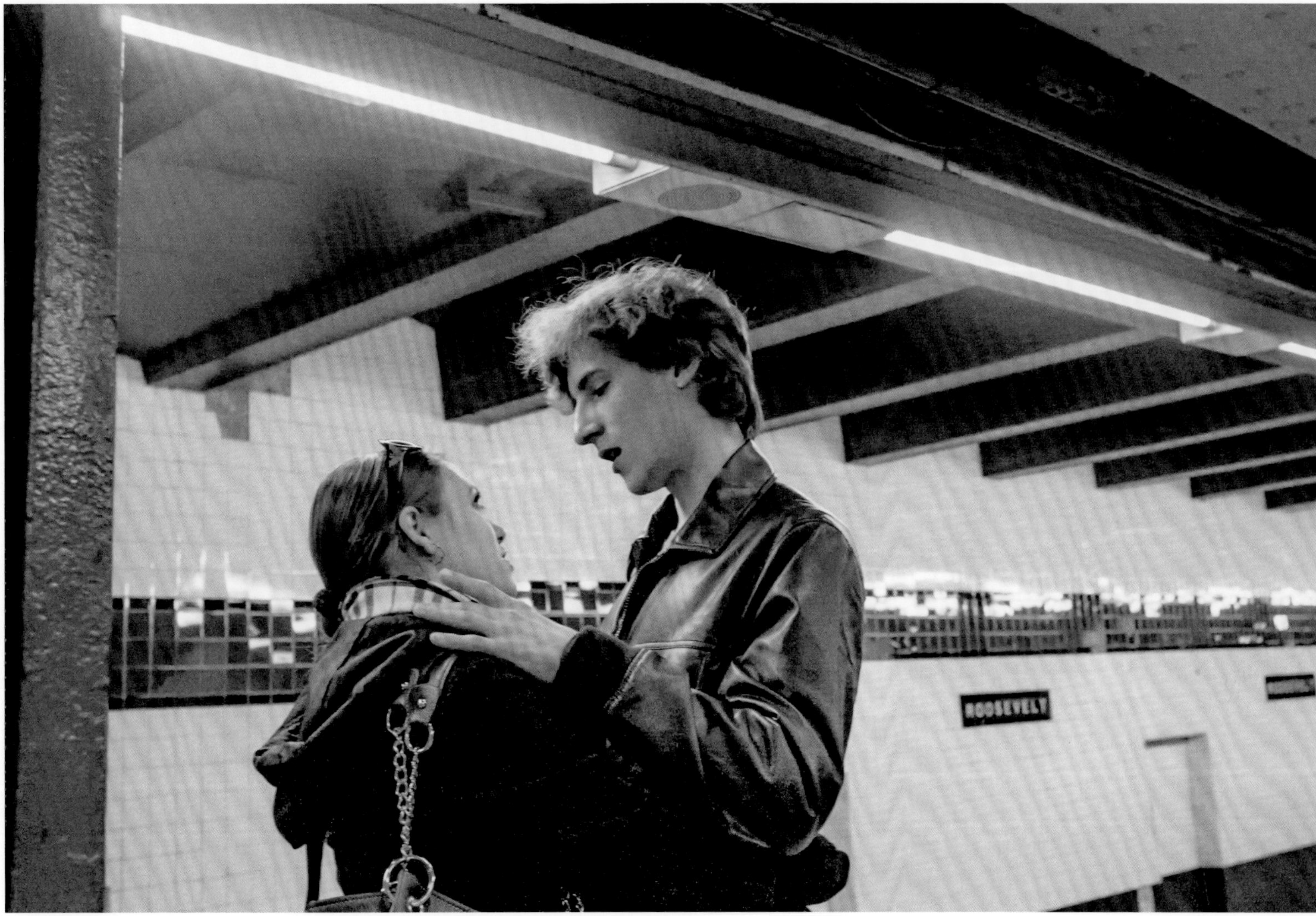

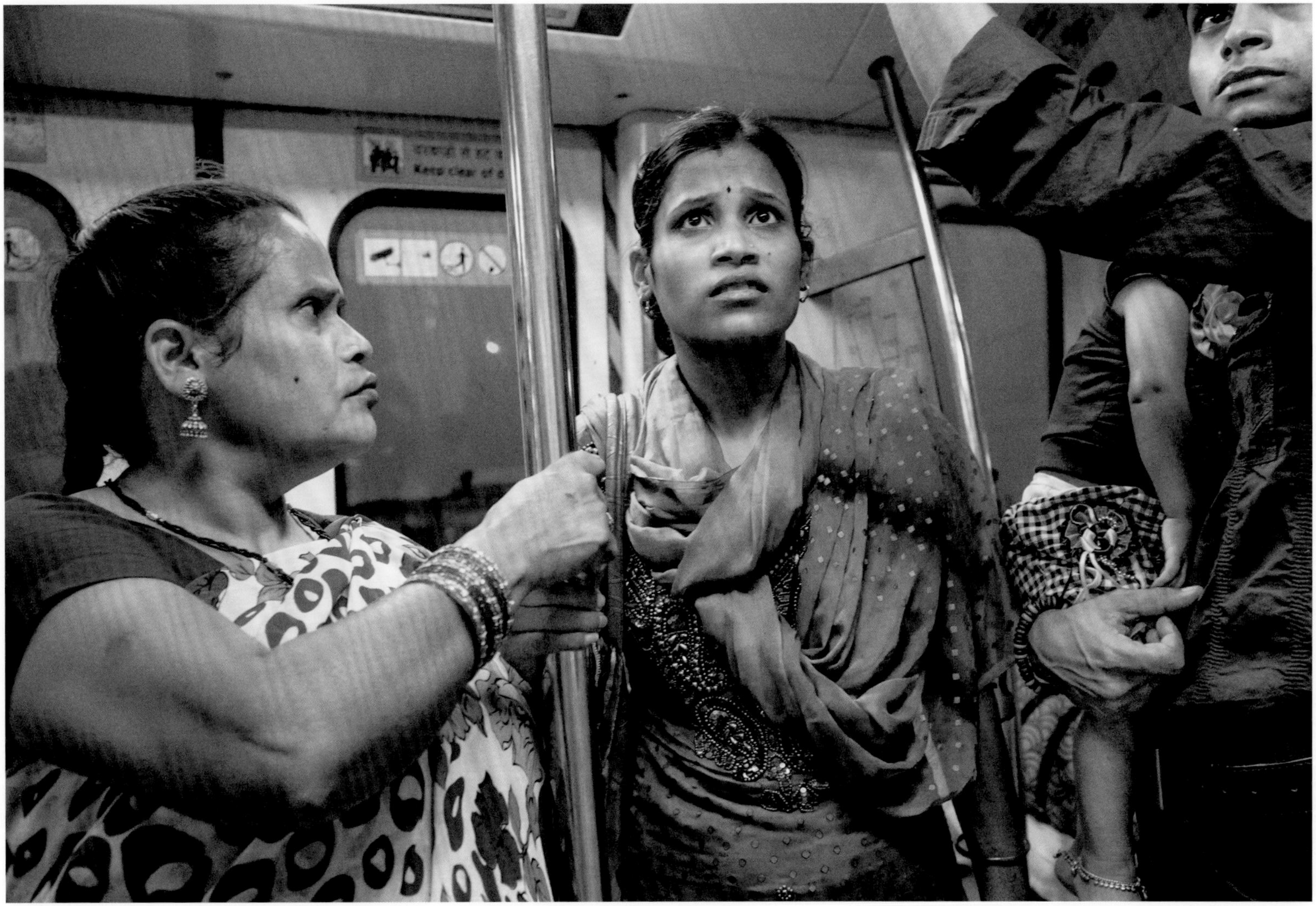

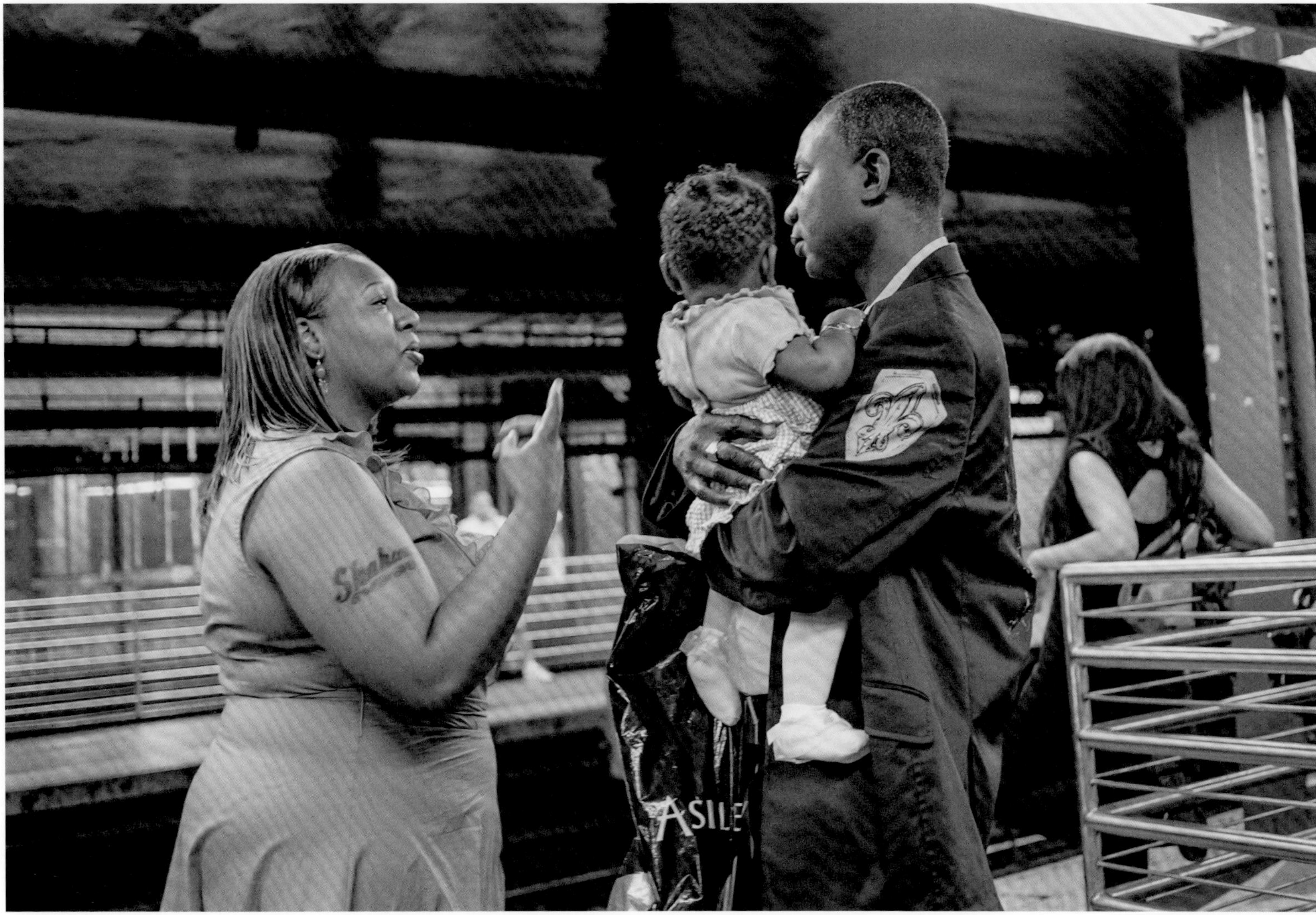

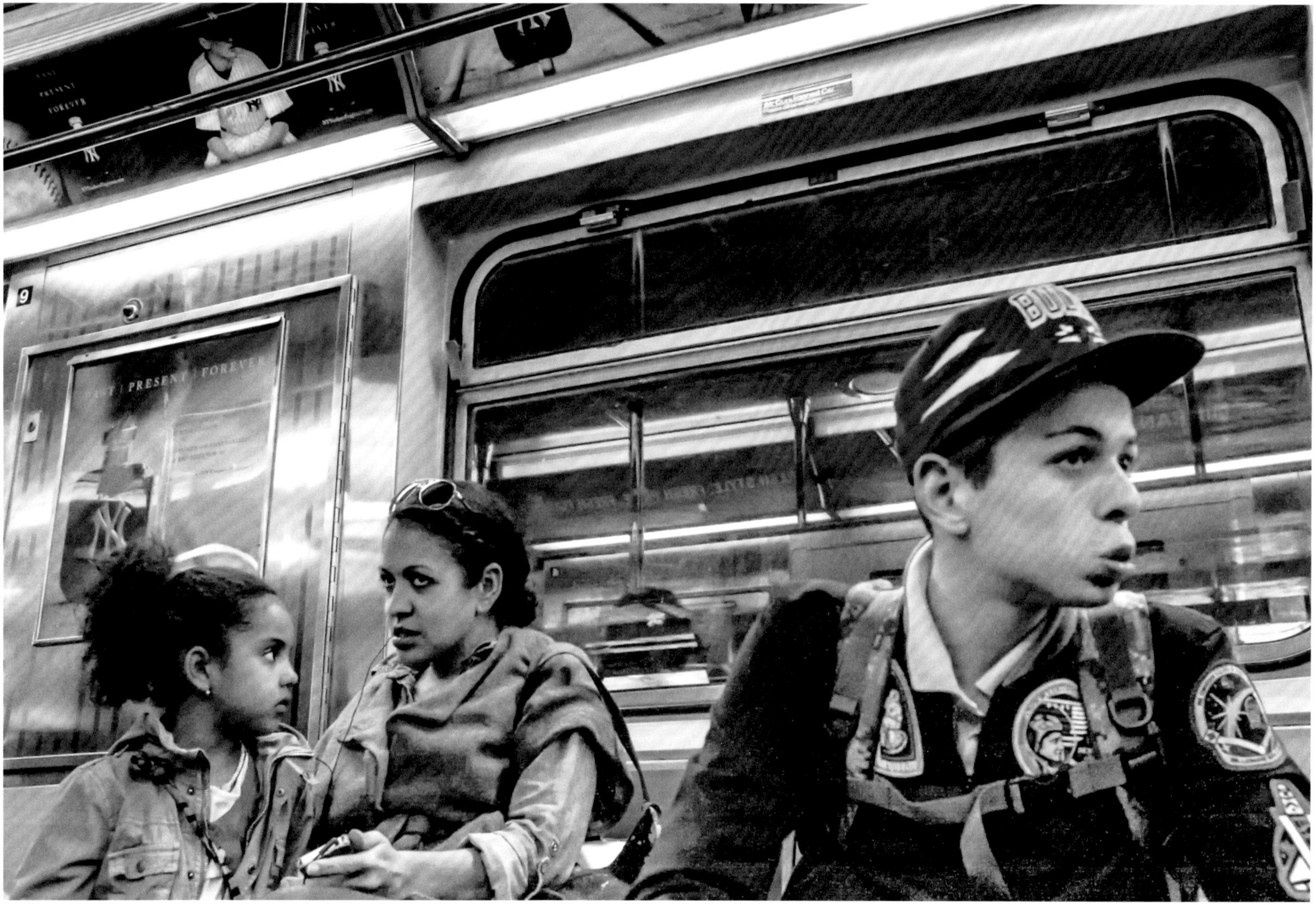
PRESENT | FOREVER

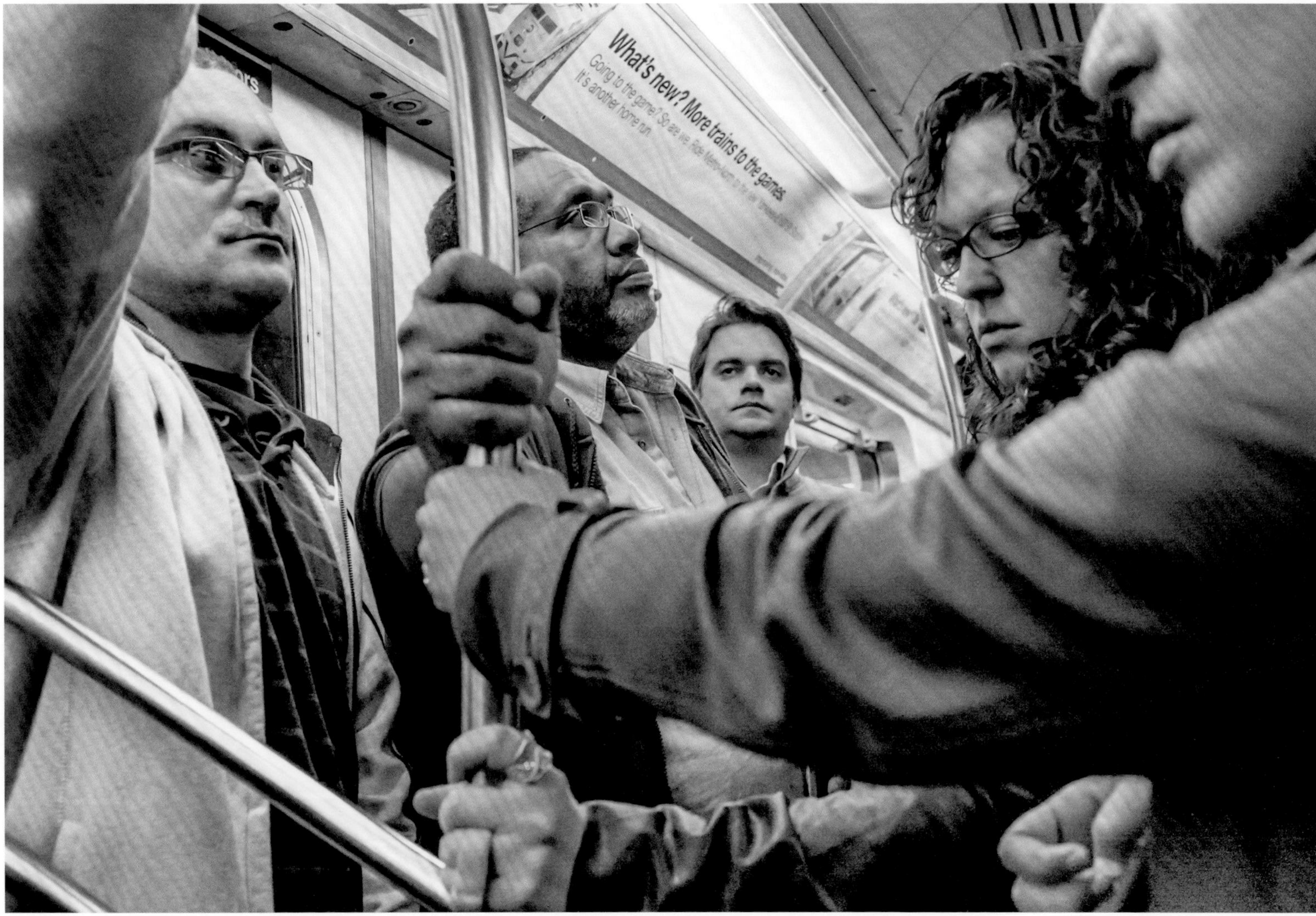
What's new? More trains to the games
It's another home run.

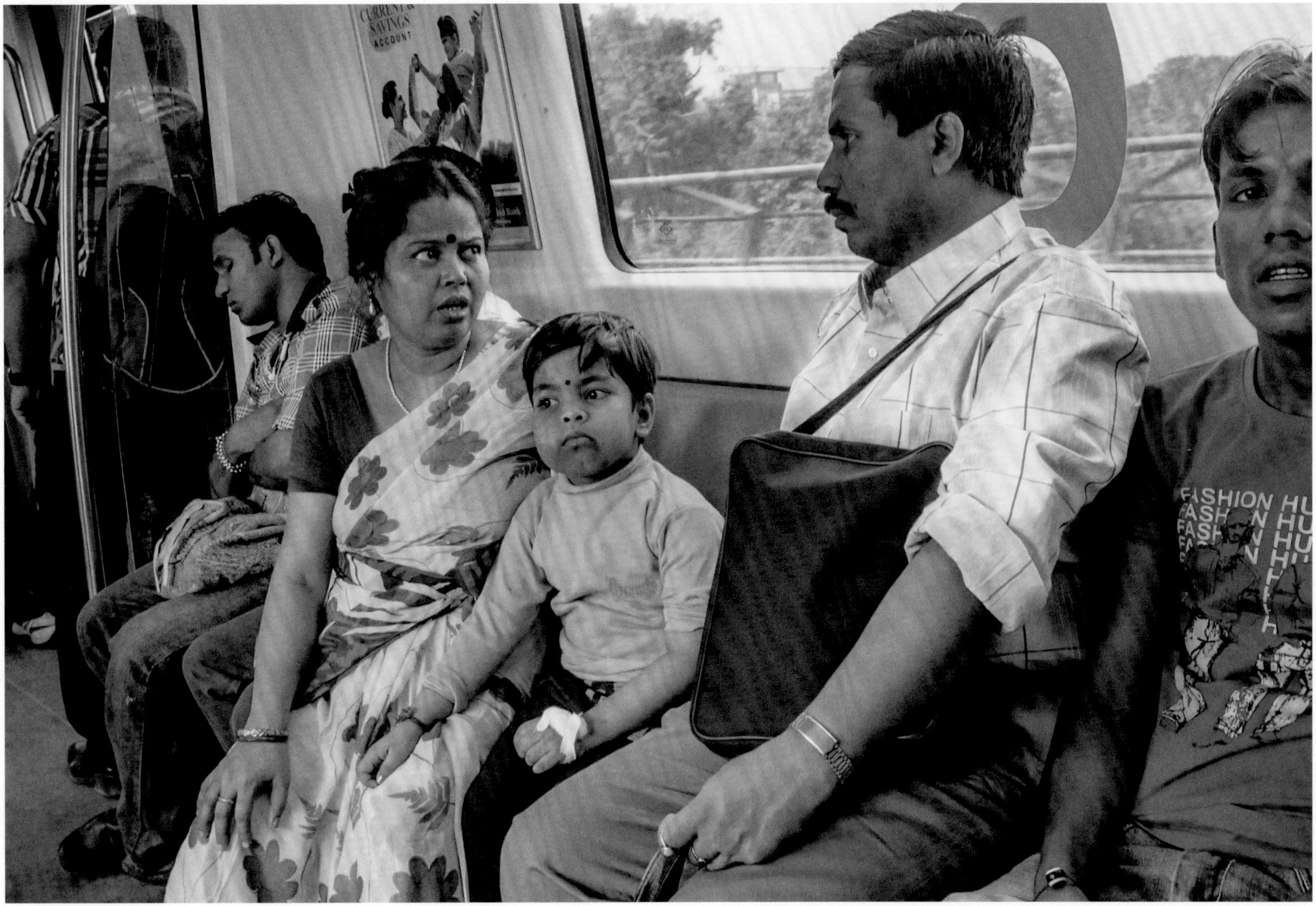
CURRENT & SAVINGS ACCOUNT

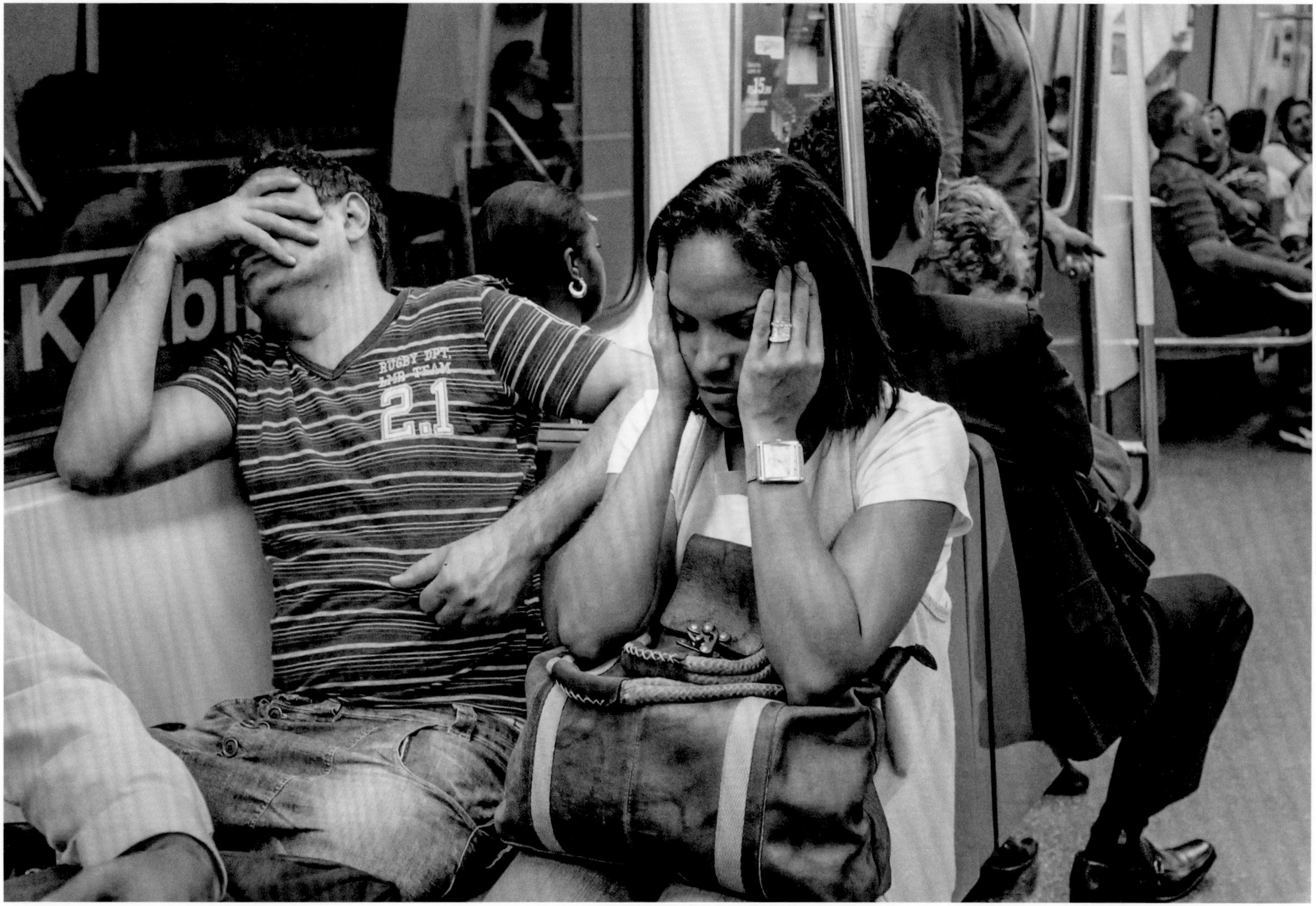
RUGBY DPT.
LMR TEAM
2.1

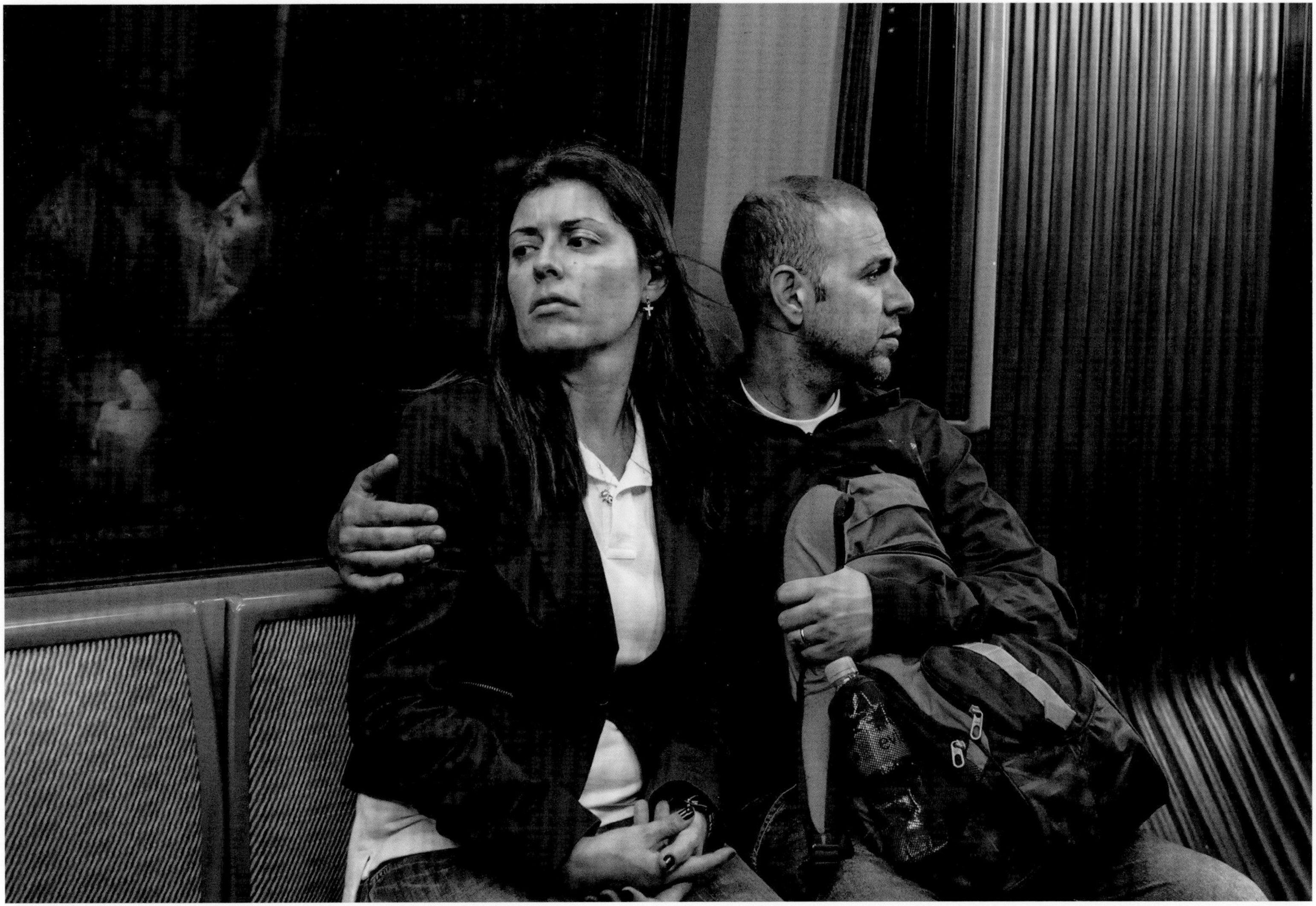

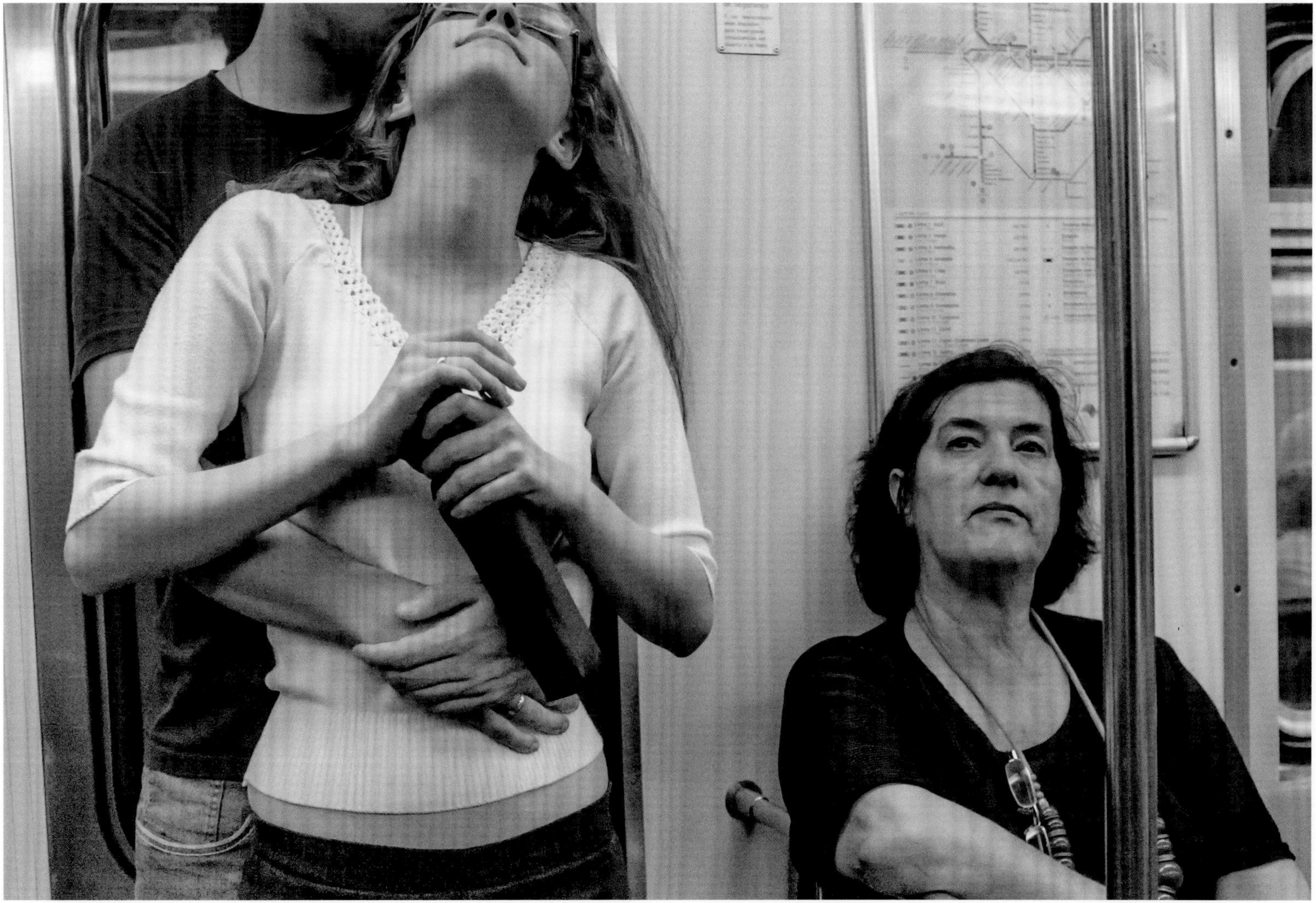

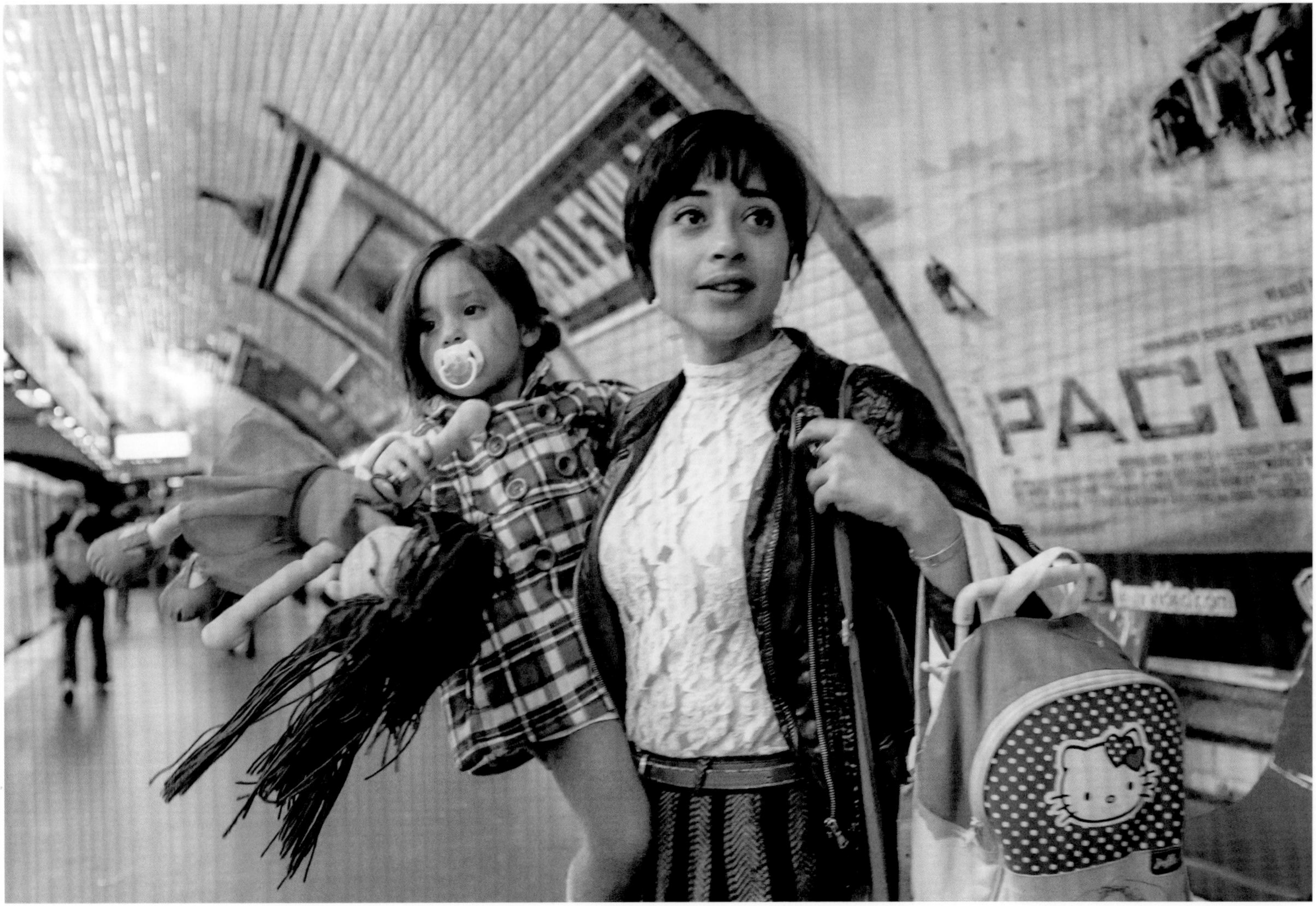
PACIF

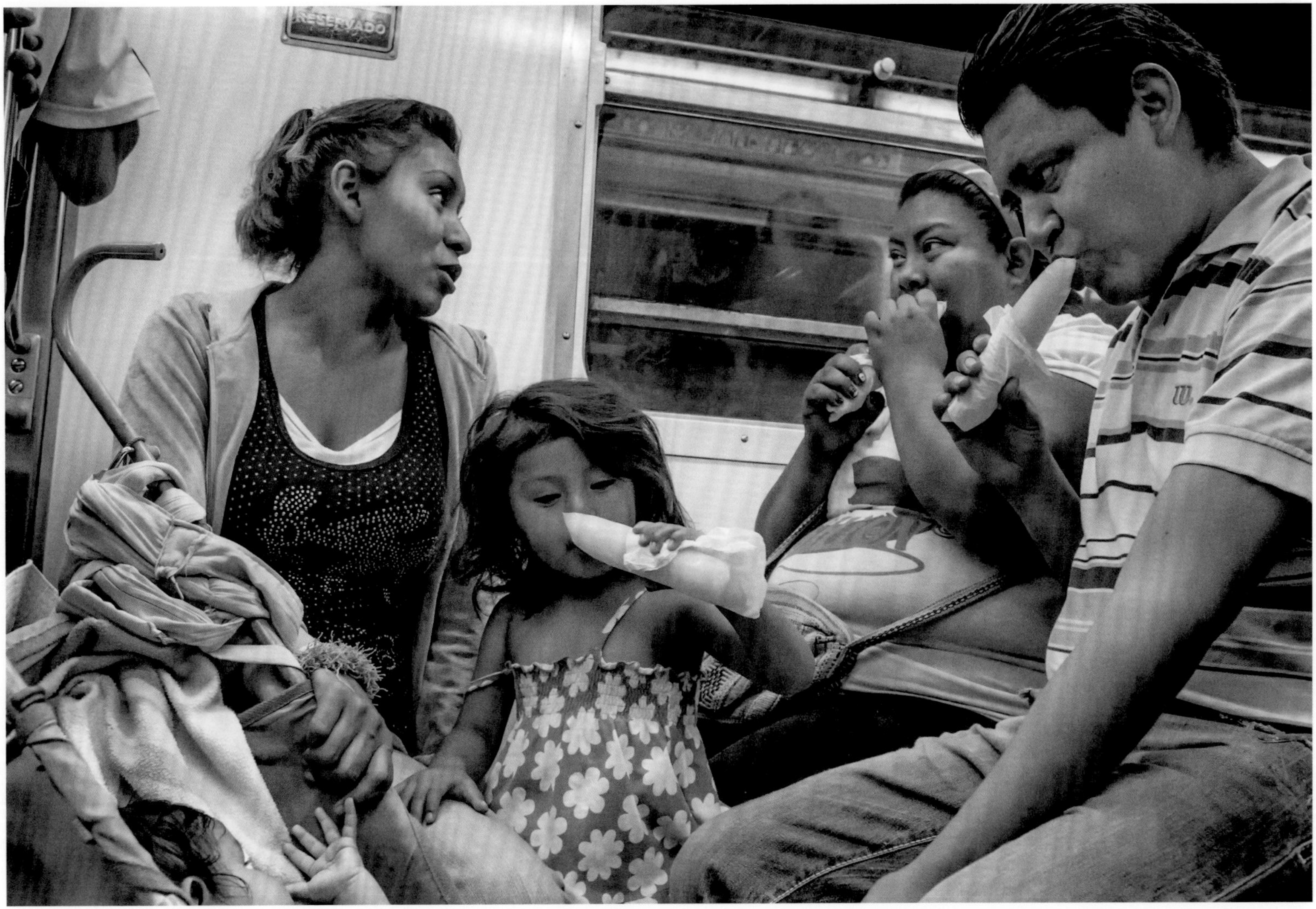
RESERVADO

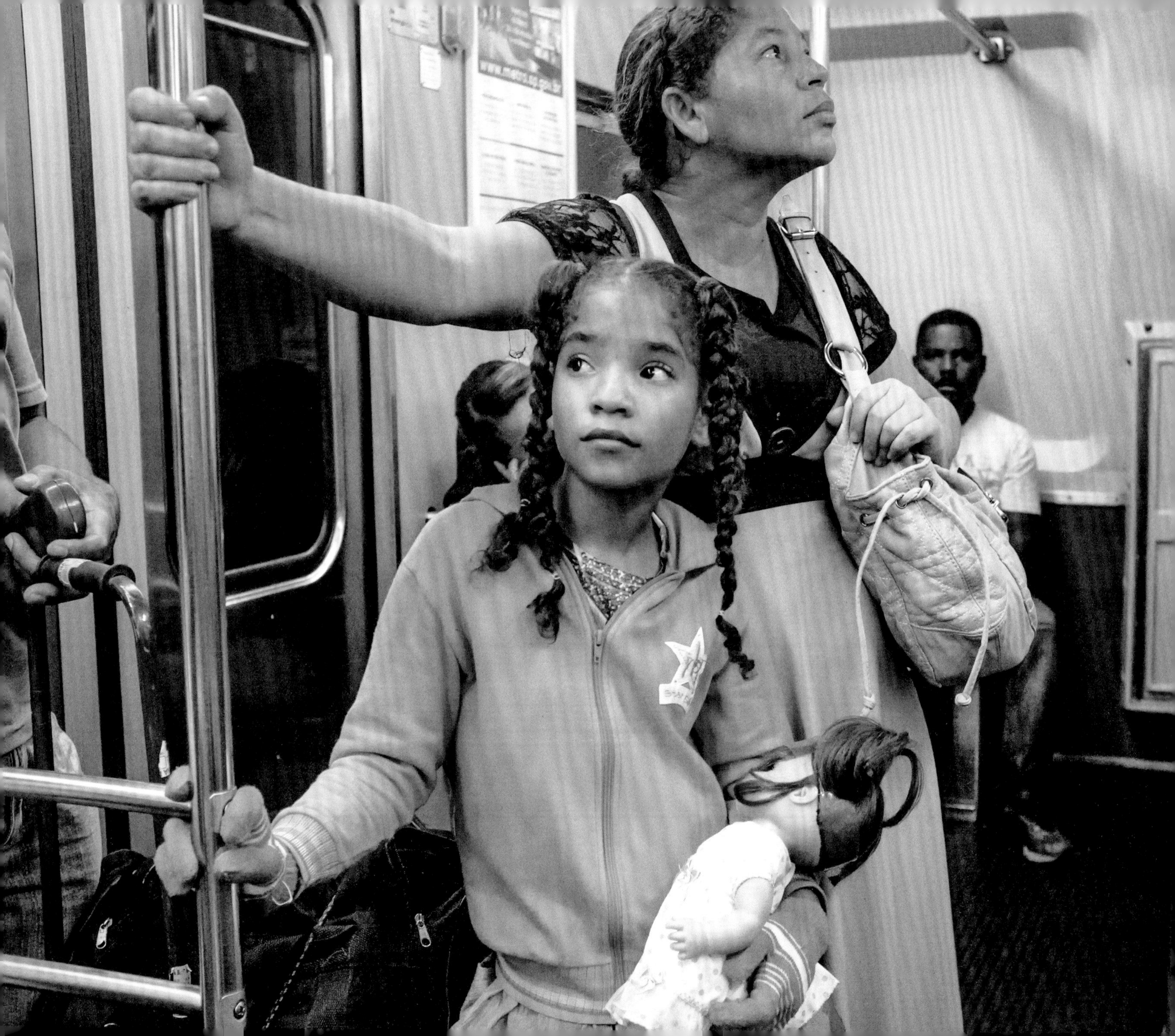

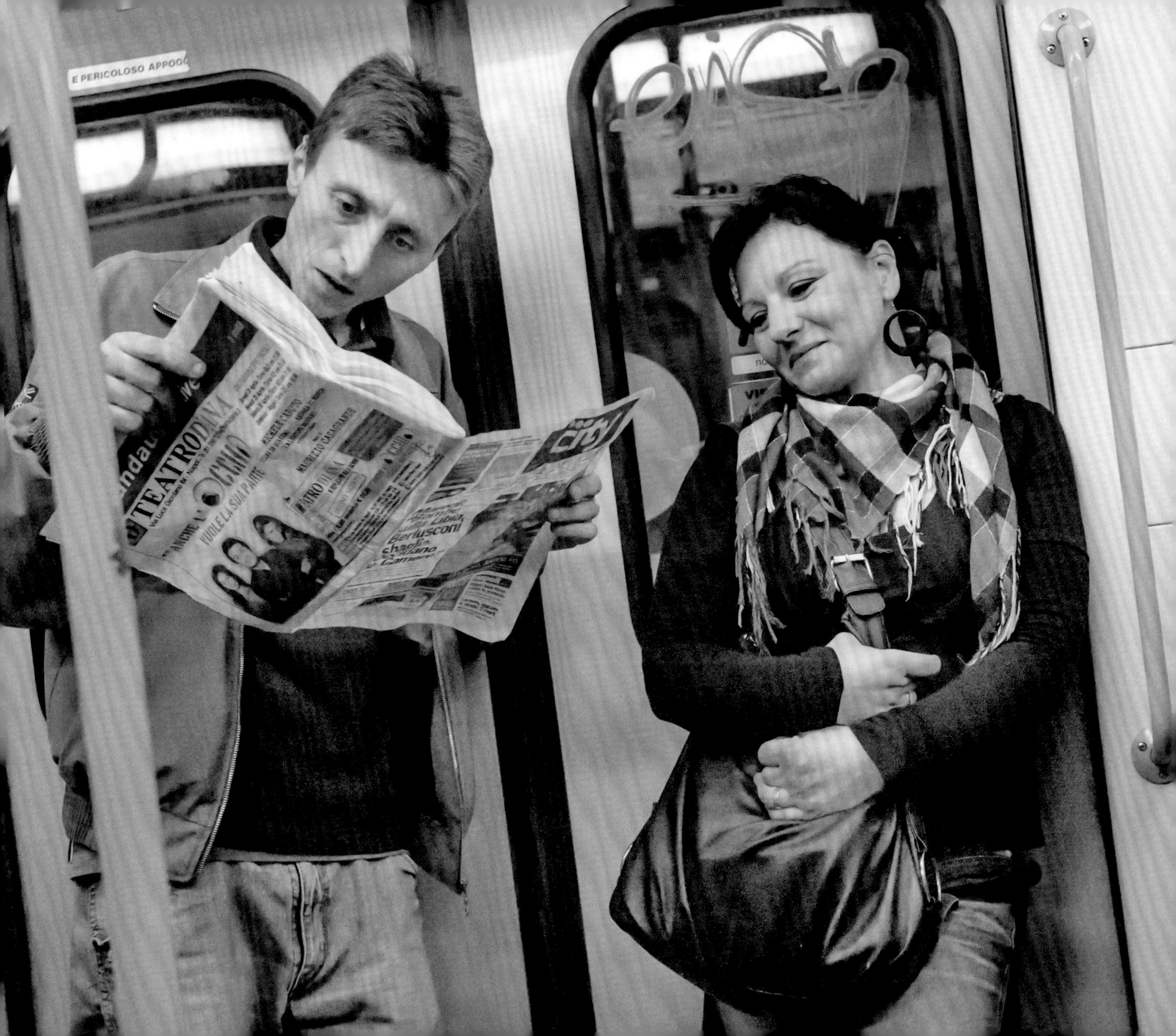
E PERICOLOSO APPOGG
TEATRODIANA
VUOLE LA SUA PARTE
MAURIZIO CASAGRANDE
city
Berlusconi

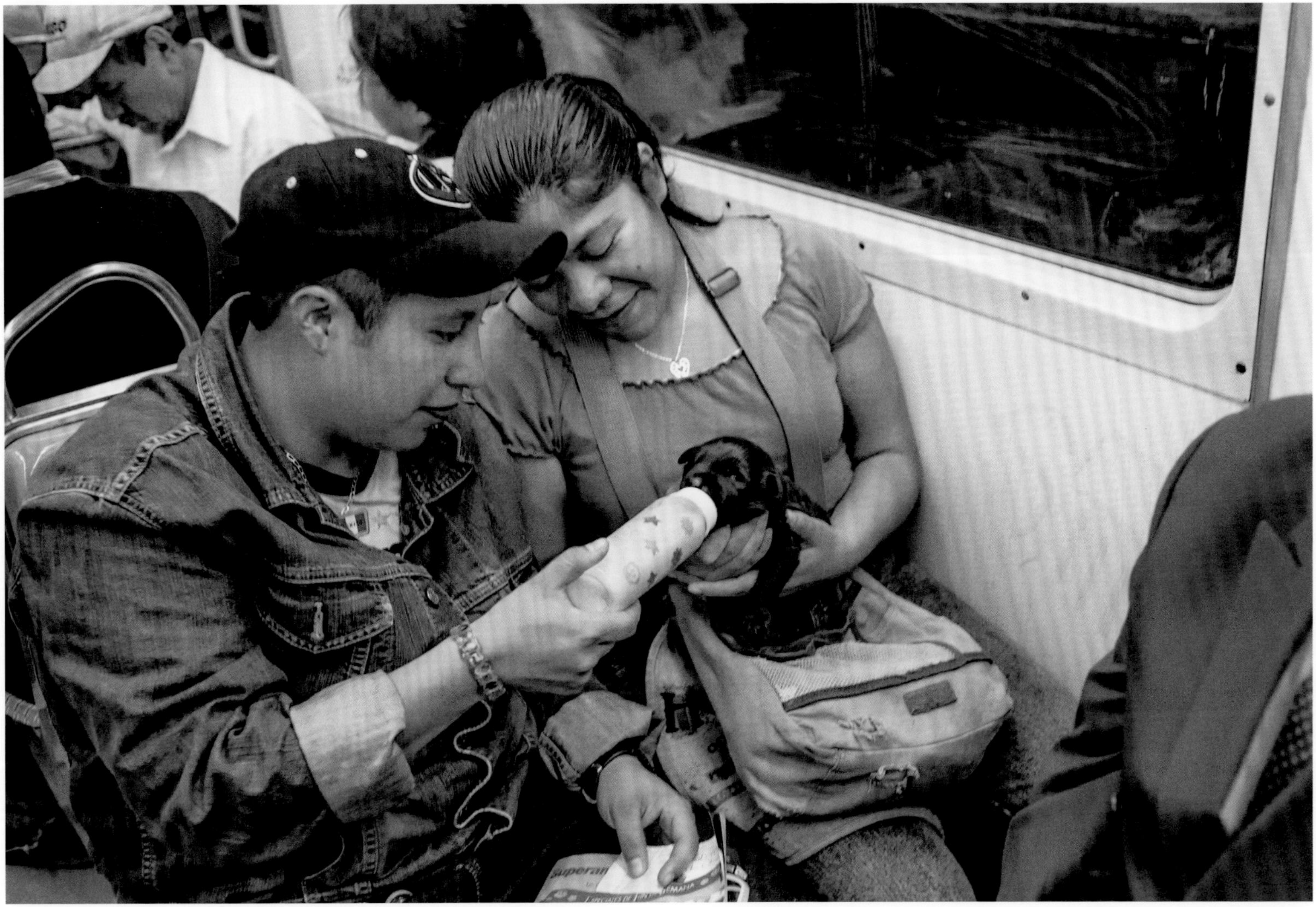

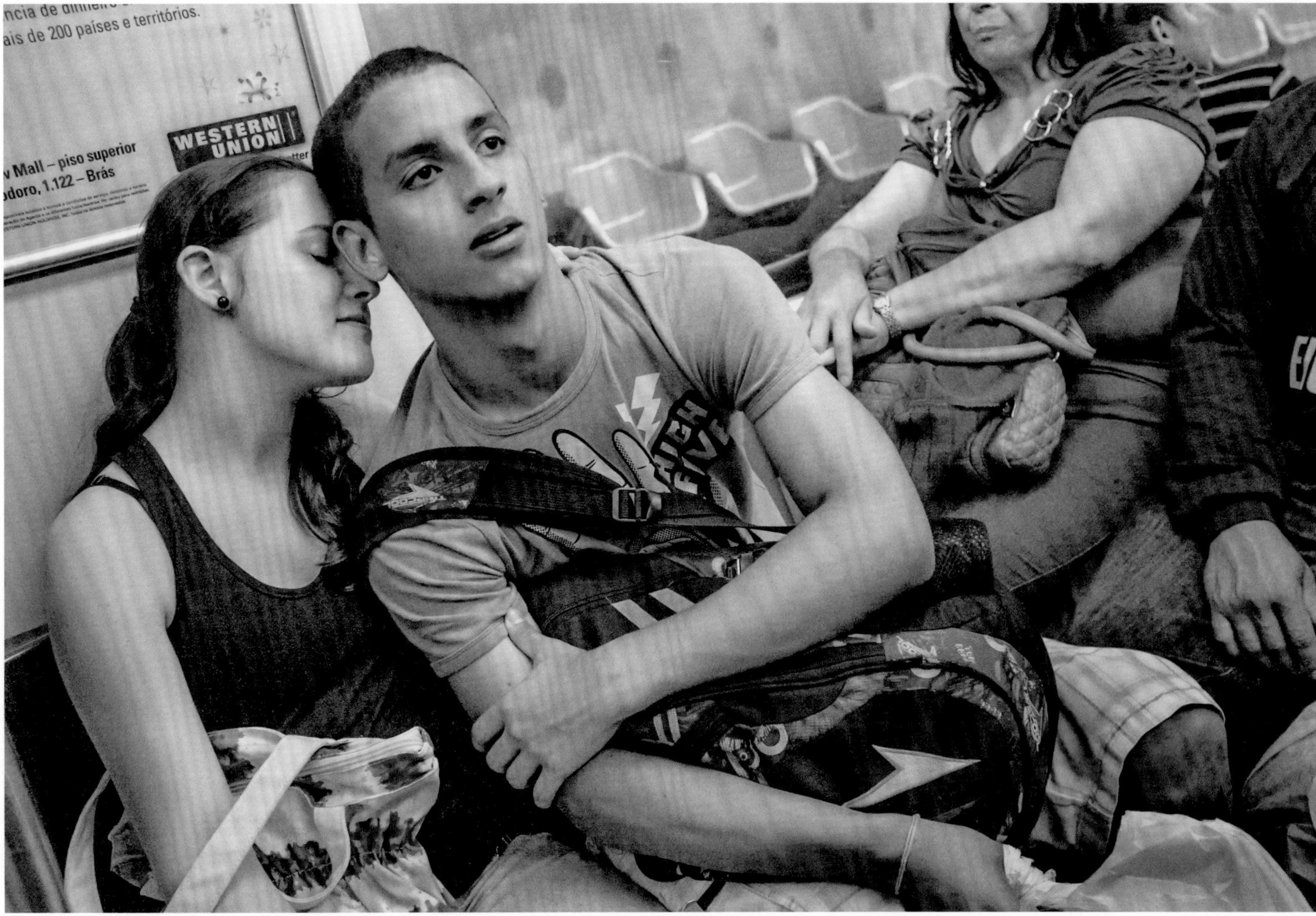
ais de 200 países e territórios.
WESTERN UNION
v Mall – piso superior
odoro, 1.122 – Brás

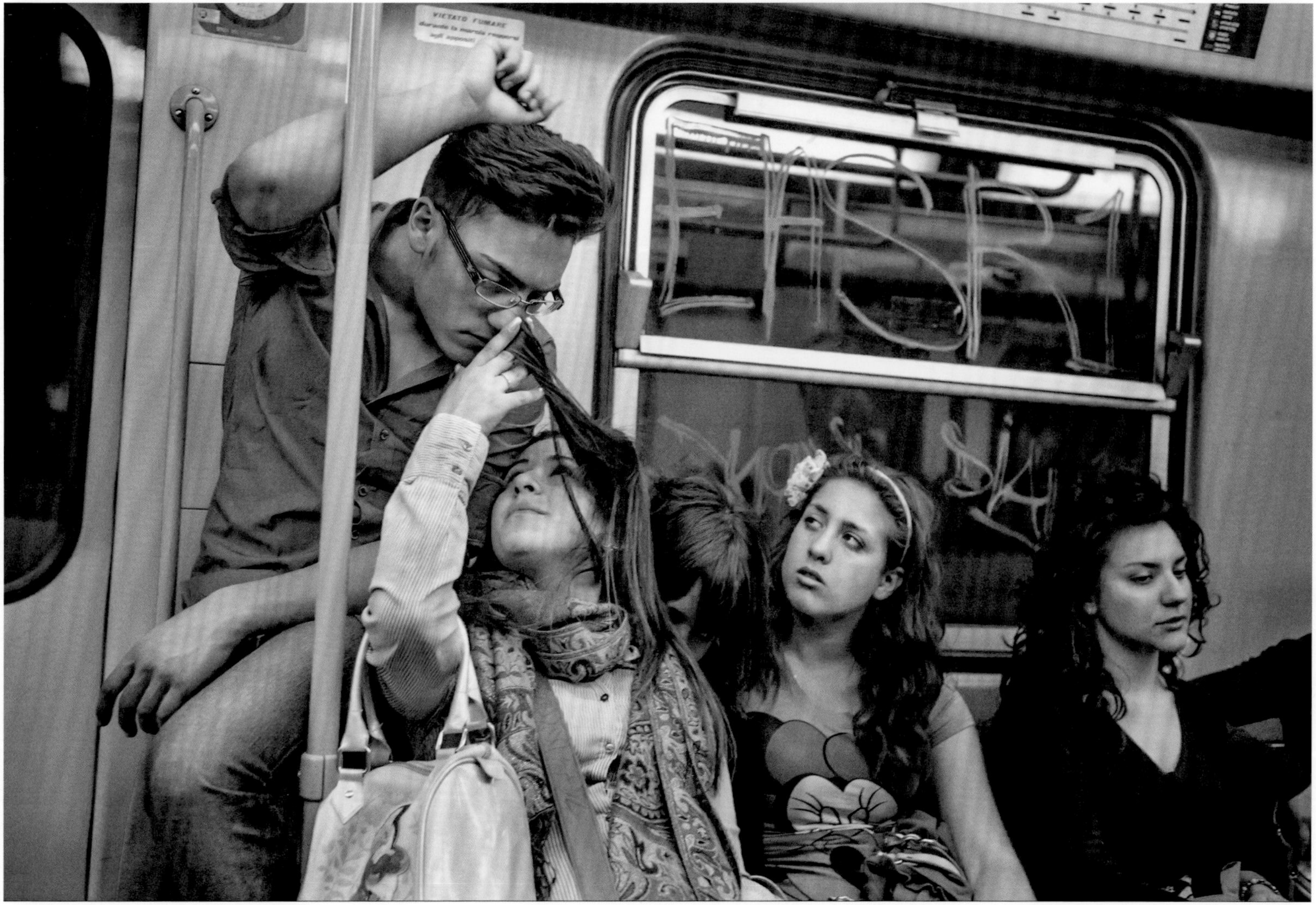
VIETATO FUMARE

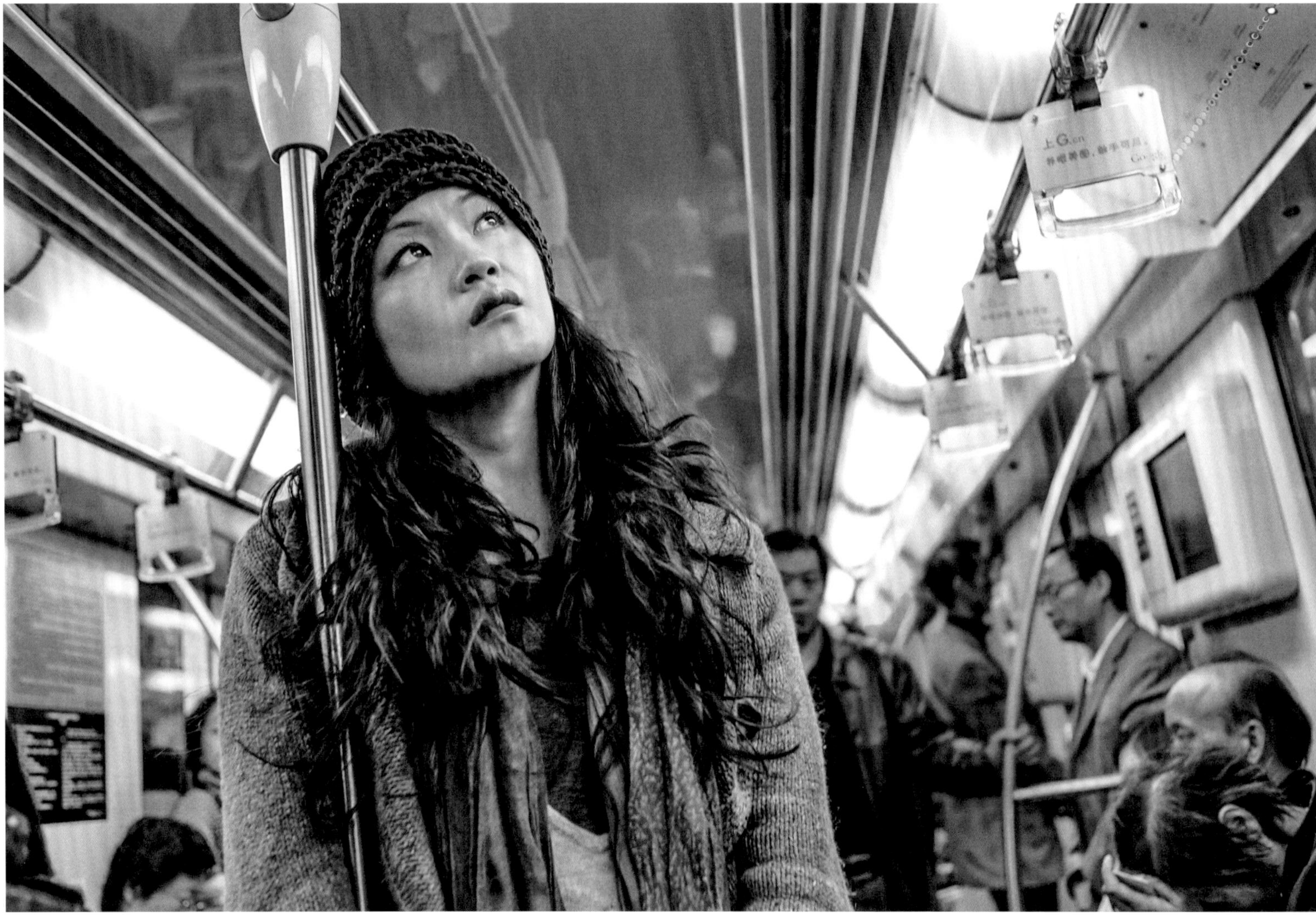

We are so small between the stars,
so large against the sky,
and lost among the subway crowds,
I try to catch your eye.

—Leonard Cohen

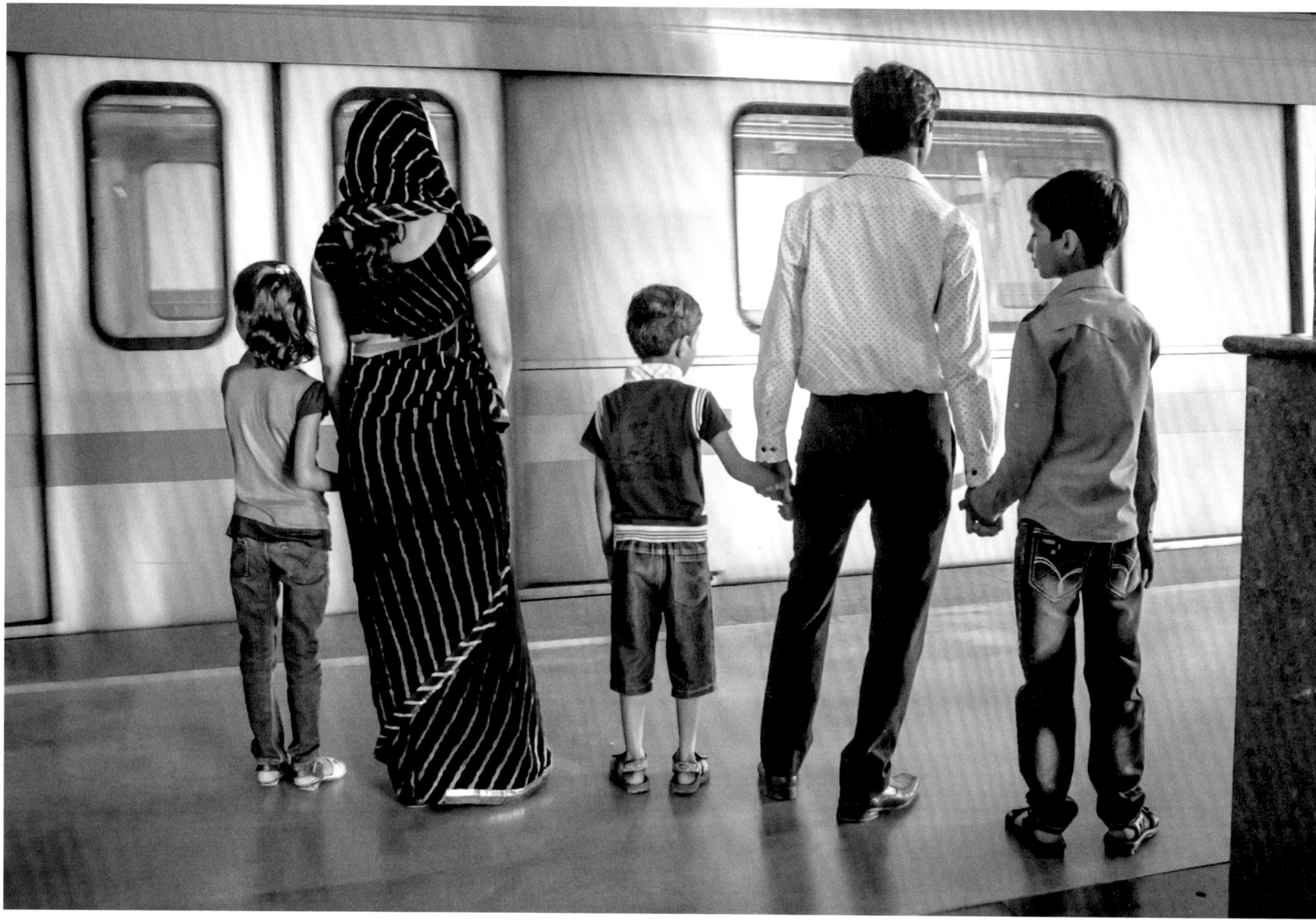

Chemistry:

1. the branch of science that deals with the identification of the substances of which matter is composed; the investigation of their properties and the ways in which they interact, combine, and change; and the use of these processes to form new substances

2. the complex emotional or psychological interaction between two people

—*Oxford Dictionary*

"Images are not merely seen but lived. They are not just vision but the cosmos itself as it expands and amplifies from the minute to the magnified."

—*Gaston Bachelard*, The Poetics of Space

The metro snakes throughout the city like a rogue strand of recombinant DNA, commanded by an unseen conductor, ceaselessly shuffling passengers. Each city's metro has its own proprietary expression, its own unspoken and spoken rules: No spitting! No smoking! No man-spreading! No eye contact!

Despite regional variations, the choreography remains much the same. The metro's doors open, and we step inside for a journey not yet written, one both shared and yet entirely our own. Amid an onslaught of stimuli, sounds, grime, advertisements, and the mushing and messing of bodies, we claim a self-carved space. If lucky, we sink into a seat and our head, reveries, preoccupations, and, perchance, conversation. We physically and mentally shift our loads, our children.

For some, the metro is a temporary temple to pore over prayer books, a haven to convene with God. For others, it's a mobile home, a place to sleep and to store a week's worth of stuff and smells while on the way to God knows where.

In and out parade the characters, the crazies, the hipsters, the tourists, the workers, the wealthy, the young, the elderly, the itinerant, and each and every one of us. We puzzle over maps, iPhones, and the unpredictability of fellow passengers. We dine. Since September 11, we fear. We apply meticulous makeup, rehearse our lines and librettos, chin ourselves on its crossbars, breakdance to beatboxes on its floors.

We photograph. We are transported.

Stan Raucher is an organic chemist by training and a photographer by love. With eight years of dedication, a chemist's rigor, and his eye, intuition, and camera, he's traversed metros shooting from London to São Paulo to Paris to Shanghai, inextricably bound with us in this roving experiment.

Raucher's focus is not the dramatic actions that usually capture our consciousness and newspaper headlines. He's not a subway Weegee. He's drawn toward moments internal and intimate, quiet and quotidian, interactions startling only in how universally commonplace—how human—they are, in how the very publicness of riding a subway can give way to moments of intimacy at all.

In one photo, a young man intently inhales strands of a young woman's hair, while the girl next to her looks on, perturbed perhaps that no one shows interest in her own, despite its large flower. A young Latino couple leans against the metro door. The girl is riveted to the barren urban landscape outside. (It's Mexico City, but it could be the Bronx or Brooklyn.) Her boyfriend speaks animatedly to someone offscreen. The botanica Jesus in his hand is swathed in amulets and beads, while his own hair is gelled like a crown of thorns. A seated family fills a frame, simultaneously enjoying *paletas*. The elongated ice pops exaggerate the vectors of their elbows and arms as the baby below reaches toward them, unnoticed. In another picture, a child peers into a darkened, reflective, and somewhat ominous train window scratched with jagged graffiti while she leans with trepidation into her mother, who seems elsewhere and entirely exhausted. Raucher's photos illuminate these fleeting connections and the fact that no one ride is ever the same for any two people—no matter how closely we are pressed together in this life.

A low-angle shot on Paris's Métro captures with synchronicity a triumvirate of faces: a seated older woman with downturned mouth turns toward a man who seems her husband. He regards her—or perhaps instead the intense eyes of the billboard siren who fills the window.

In Shanghai, a beautiful Asian woman, wrapped in a white fur like an unattainable gift, peers up, perhaps at a map, while the suited man adjacent looks on wistfully, his hand cupping his chin. Perhaps he deliberates how to make contact; perhaps he regrets he'll never have the nerve. It's these narratives we create from the elements the photographer links in his camera lens that are at the heart of Raucher's images.

In many ways, Raucher's *Metro* is reminiscent of the "pure observation" documentaries of filmmaker Frederick Wiseman, who so unobtrusively contemplates the daily interplay of his subjects in seemingly mundane details that build to powerful stories. Much like Wiseman's *Boxing Gym* and *ZOO*, Raucher's *Metro* is rooted firmly in geography, daily routine, democracy (the metro may be as democratic as our societies get), and, especially, in the editing.

Raucher finds parallels between photo editing and the practice of organic chemistry. "Synthesizing complex organic molecules," he says, "provides a good analogy to sequencing a photo book. There are countless different ways to go about this, and the final results bear the distinctive signature of the scientist or artist."

As a photographer, a chemist, and an editor, Raucher explores the tangible and intangible matter that binds us, and he reveals many discoveries. It's interesting that Gaston Bachelard, who so carefully contemplated the poetics of space, was himself a chemist before becoming a philosopher.

To be transported is to be moved, both physically and emotionally, to allow oneself to be taken somewhere, in some ways to be filled with faith and promise. *Metro* is reflective of Raucher's own faith in humanity, and a belief that these goings-on beneath the surface of our streets, in the subways, are somehow emblematic of those everyday molecular interactions that occur unseen before us yet are so integral to life itself.

Raucher's images explore and magnify a self-contained world. Yet rather than contain ours, they enable us to see farther, both into the metro and into ourselves.

—Marlaine Glicksman

I'd like to thank Michael Itkoff and Taj Forer for their enthusiastic support, Ursula Damm for her wonderful design and unwavering patience, Elizabeth Bell for her copyediting, and everyone at Daylight Books.

I'm delighted that Ed Kashi, my online mentor for my 2010 Lucie Foundation award, brought this project full circle by writing the foreword. Thanks also to Marlaine Glicksman for entwining aspects of art, science, and my past and current endeavors in her essay.

I'm grateful for the inspiration and guidance I've received from all of the mentors and friends I've met on my photographic journey, with particular gratitude to Mary Ellen Mark and Ernesto Bazan. Thanks also to Laura Moya and Laura Valenti of Photolucida, and to everyone at Blue Sky Gallery.

This project was a 2012 CDS/Honickman First Book Prize in Photography finalist, so I would like to thank Alexa Dilworth and the Center for Documentary Studies at Duke University. Thanks to Brooks Jensen for including some of these images in LensWork #97, and to Aline Smithson for featuring this project in Lenscratch.

Special thanks to Victoria Bjorklund and Ron Hammond for their helpful suggestions and assistance. Finally, to all of my friends and family, who may have thought that I disappeared somewhere underground during the preparation of this book, thank you!

—Stan Raucher

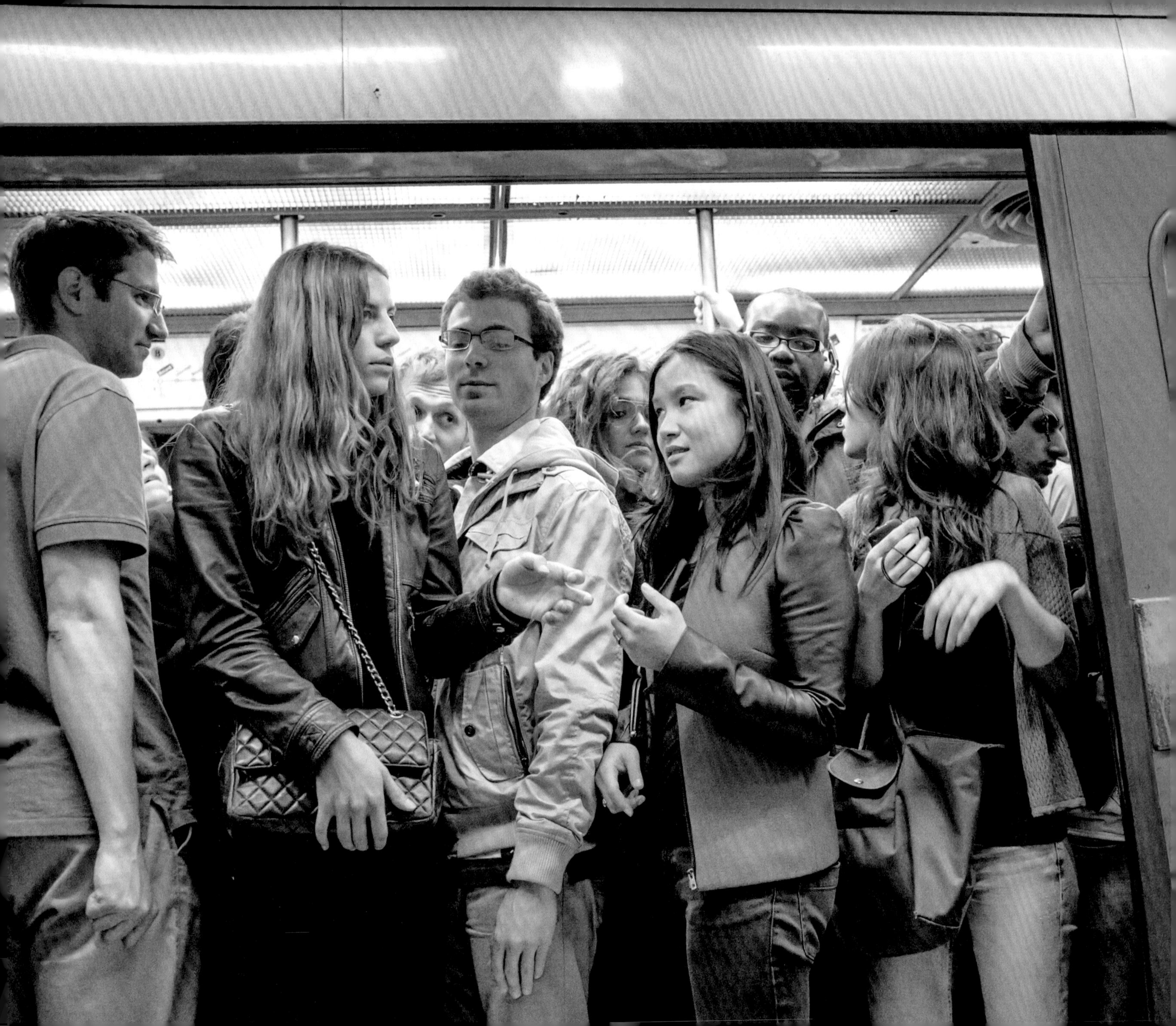